**The Road to UTOPIA**
(and how to take a short cut)


Author: 2 x Global Entrepreneur 'Big Impact to Business' Award Winner
Jay Allen

ISBN-13: 978-1539743309

ISBN-10: 1539743306

## Dedication

This book is primarily dedicated to all those who are still searching for their WHY! Their purpose. Who have a dream, vision, but have yet to establish a clear and focused set of goals to achieve it.

# Contents

## Acknowledgements

Firstly, to Mr. Ramond Aaron, New York Times Number one published Author, international keynote speaker, colleague, and friend. My thanks for giving me the inspiration, encouragement and means to publish my first book 'Battlefield2Boardroom – 10 Proven Military Methods to Combat Mediocrity' You have lit the touch paper to my inspiration as an author – Thank you.

Secondly to my friend Adam Kara, for being you! From your moment of inspiration during Mastermind to the launch of your next highly successful business, from audacious targets and unbelievable time scales, from not listening to anyone else but your gut and your instinct and for not being swayed by anyone.
Your forward to this book sets the tone for the following pages!

Thirdly, all my current and previous clients within My TrueNORTH for the trust, faith and belief in me and my aims for you all. I continue to be inspired by you, your businesses, your drive and determination, your vision, your goals, and your ambitions.

Finally to you as a reader, thank you for picking up this book cover and choosing to spend some of your most valuable time with me, I assure you I value time immensely and most grateful you would spend some of yours with me.

Foreward

Let's assume for one minute that your lifelong quest was to make it to the North Pole! Although this might sound absurd to you right now, just bear with me as everything shall soon become apparent!

You recognize that to achieve this you simply can't jump on a flight and visit for the weekend, so you'll have to trek! To do so you're going to need a series of things:

•       TRAINING – It's highly unlikely you'll ever get there successfully unless you have first conducted some training, maybe achieved a mountain leader's qualification, carried out some practice to prepare you for the journey ahead.
•       TEAM – It's also highly unlikely you're going to achieve this on your own. So perhaps sourcing, selecting and effectively communicating with the right people that are going to support, assist, encourage and motivate you to achieve this momentous goal.
•       EQUIPMENT – However it's going to be impossible to trek from where you are right now and reach the North Pole without equipment! The right clothing, the right type of shelter, food and of course a damn good compass!

So, you've conducted all your training, you've selected a great team of people, bought all the necessary equipment, including a highly recommended compass, waited for the needle to settle over the N and set out to religiously follow its direction; RIGHT?.......
...WRONG!

Set out from the UK and follow the N, and you'll find yourself somewhere in SCANDINAVIA! You see your following MAGNETIC NORTH! To get to the North Pole, you'd have to offset the compass by approx. 11degree's to compensate for the various magnetic impulses around the northern hemisphere which would otherwise guide you off course, but unless you knew this, your always (regardless of the best intent) going to fail to achieve what you set out to achieve!

However, if only it were that simple! You see, set off from anywhere in the southern hemisphere, and you've got a whole host of other magnetic impulses determining you can't just rely on the 11-degree offset rule! Compensate for these and your STILL unlikely to achieve it! You see as the earth revolves in its orbit, on its axis around the sun, the North Pole does not stay stationary! But rather moves in loops of up to 50 miles (80 km) per day! Its actual location, an average of all these loops, is also moving at around 25 miles a year predominantly affected by global human intervention!

One of the ways you may have chosen to achieve your target, is to actually follow the lines of longitude on a map, as the flow from the South Pole to the North Pole, these lines do not deviate from their course, nor are they influenced by magnetic pulses, and are a sure way of guiding you to achieving to goal of quest to get to the North Pole – TRUE NORTH.

Exactly can be said for the majority of people who start their own business! They originally have a goal of what they aim to achieve.

They either have qualifications or experience in a certain 'thing' and rally around to get the support of either friends and family,
Colleagues or employees and they buy all the 'right equipment' be that stock or resource, be that the latest phone with a gazillion apps or the slickest laptop with more memory than a country!
And set out to achieve that shiny goal of success, be that a multi- million pound international business, or the time freedom to bring up a family, travel the world, do 'other stuff' or both!

But the mass majority of business owners are failing! Failing ever to achieve what they originally set out to achieve, and this book explains why, and how, as well as helps you understand what you can do to re-align you and your business back towards your original goals, back towards YOUR TrueNORTH!

**Jay Allen**
Founder
My TrueNORTH - The Ethical Coaching Company

And my sincerest of thanks to my good friend Adam Kara, for these words of inspiration:

*"**I love entrepreneurs.** We are a different breed of human. We have a different level of ambition and self-belief. It drives us to do things others wouldn't and take risks, which sometimes put you in a lonely place. When the going gets tough, we have a different level of grit. We have a growth mind set, learn fast, play to our strengths and compensate for our weaknesses. We see opportunity where others see nothing; we see possibility where others see impossibility. We take action to make dreams and vision's a reality. We conjure courage where fear paralyses others... or we feel the fear and do it anyway... Say screw it, push comfort zones and test our limits.*

*We lead, we manage, we solve problems, we add value, and we break the rules. We change the way the game is played, and we inspire.*

*We do all this for what?? For the money? Maybe...*
*To prove something to others? Sometimes...*

*To prove something to ourselves? ... I'd like to think so... but sadly that's probably a lie.*

*We do it because we saw the world for what it was, didn't subscribe to mediocrity and chose to do something about it. Life is too short and time is the most important thing you will ever have.*

*"Work hard at school, so you can get a good job, try harder at your job so you can get promoted to a role where you work 60 hours a week so you can get a good house and be a slave to your mortgage. Never see your friends, family... No time for yourself.*
*To live for the weekend (at best) but more likely to go on a two week holiday to feel real for a change. To be a cog in a wheel of someone else's dream."*

*It's not good enough for us.*

*We see the pain, the suffering and the waste of life that the rat race is and we called it out.*

We dared to dream, and we said "do you know what???? It's better to give it ago and fail than to never know".

We don't live a life of regret. We don't sit around and wait for someone else to make our lives better. We go out there and take full responsibility for everything that happens to us... the good, the bad, the ugly, the stress, the success, the challenges and the rewards.

We don't fear failure.......... we fear waking up one day.... many years from now and wondering what if?????????

We make decisions, and we decided to live a life of meaning, fulfillment, and PURPOSE. We dared to believe that we could make a dent in the universe and leave a legacy. Become someone. An identity by design... a lifestyle by design... to live deliberately on our terms!!!

"To spend a few years doing what most won't so we can spend the rest of lives doing what most can't..."

We are as brave as we are foolish, ambitious as we are discontent. We have a touch of genius with a splash of madness, an air of arrogance with a cool calm confidence and yet for all our good points we are deep thinkers with a dark side. We have a secret... that at any time... we can push the self-destruct button.

What if I'm not good enough?

What if I am successful and then lose it?

What will people think of me if I'm much richer and happier than them?

Why do I deserve so much when so many live with so little?

We have demons, each one of us. 'Head shit' which we battle with. We could choose to leave it behind, squash it and move on but there's a strange comfort it dancing with it... inviting it in and wondering if you can stare it straight in the eye and win this time...

*...*

*...*

*...*

*but you don't.*

*...*

*It never gives in.*

*Is entrepreneurship a gift or a curse...?*

*Is it inevitable that we feel this way OR is that what secretly drives us?*

*The pain of staying the same is more than the pain of change?*

*Is this the dark before the dawn? The sign that change is coming? When you need to step it up a gear?*

*The uncertainty of tomorrow drives me forward to determine my future; I am not shackled by the constraints of employment or the establishment; I am an entrepreneur."*

## Chapter One - It all starts with a DREAM

You all must be familiar with the word *"Utopia"* right? If not, let me first share with you what *"Utopia"* actually means. *"Utopia"* is where EVERYTHING is perfect or an imagined place or state, in which everything is perfect.

When you read the Term *"Imagination,"* *"An Imagined Place"* or *"State."* Every one of us has our imaginations or imagined places where you have set out everything, everything that you wish to have is aligned and available right at your disposal but with the passage of time and growth, you simply forget this place and start to believe it isn't possible.

You start to train your brain to move or walk on a certain path, a certain way which leads you to a full stop, an end where your Utopia ends with a Red Sign written on it *"Impossible"*, *"Not Possible"*, *"You can't do it"*, *"It's out of your Limits"* and you end there. You live the normal life of waking up, going to School/College/Work, eating, hanging out and sleeping creating a mediocrity called reality and thus pushing Utopia into the closet, away from view and certainly not to be considered on a regular basis!

There are times, though, where you still have momentary Utopias! You see a fancy car and think, "*What if I had it?*" You see someone with a precisely tailored suit worn by a person having a charming personality, and you think "*What If I was the one that had worn this precisely tailored suit and had a charming suit where everywhere I go everyone greets me with respect?*" You see that is where you fall, that is where you raise a Red Flag on your Utopia, that is where you start following the path, which leads to the end of your Utopia. Do you begin to think, "*How can I be like him? How can I have that fancy car, that Fancy Suit and what not?*" And you end up calming down your motivational level from inspirational until it comes back to Zero and you go on back to your 'Normal Life'.

You must have seen extraordinary people in your Life, right? Someone that has been successful, someone that has been enjoying every bit of his/her life and you are just wondering to yourself as to how can you be like him/her.

You see we have a problem with our perceptions; we start to believe and think like the way that our norms and culture teaches us, what our society teaches us. We just think, we just imagine, we only allow ourselves momentary short time perceptions. We don't have a Vision, a long term 24/7 vision of seeing things through, a Vision of bringing our "*Utopia*" to life, making it come to being, and this is the first failure to achieve! You see EVERY successful person that you see around the globe has their Utopias too; but have trained their minds to eradicate failure, mediocre, uncertainty or doubt and replaced with a living utopia!

Had they said to themselves "*It couldn't be done?*" Had they raised a red flag to their "*Utopia*" Things would have been extremely different, but NO! They never did. They believed in themselves. They never trusted a single thought of it can't happen; I can't do it! They believed right from the start in themselves and believed in bringing their "*Utopia*" to Life. Everyone has heard of Steve Jobs, right? But are you aware HOW he created the Multi-million-dollar company Apple? Just with a magic wand and **Kaboom** Here's his overnight success company? NO! He started in a garage, his garage, just like you and I have garage's in our home. He started there on the workshop table, but from right there he already believed in changing the world with his great Idea. He trusts his "*Utopia*," despite struggling and having troubles, disbelief, and challenges he continued with his belief until he CREATED UTOPIA.

If Steve has done it, (Bill Gates, Richard Branson, Elon Musk) why can't you? None of them were born with special powers, non-born into the companies they created; they didn't have any other special qualities more than you.

However, they are living proof that dreaming, believing, trusting, in following *"The Road to their Utopia"* and then making it become a reality.

The Journey of a thousand miles begins with the first step.

You got a business idea? Good. Let's make it work. Your initial thought most probably would be, *"Nah I'm building on it. It is bound to fail in the raw form it is in now. I need to refine it and come up with something more tangible that has a 100% certainty of success"*. Truth be told you will never get there. You can never work out an idea so much as to say it is an impeccable piece among the millions of business ventures floating about.

It is you and only you who can dictate terms and guide it to the triumph it deserves.

**What holds us back?**

Surely you want to start the business you always dreamt about. Everyone yearns to turn that brilliant inkling that constantly echoes in their minds into something more tangible. Who doesn't want to turn the idea of that killer product that will change millions of lives into reality?
So what is it that keeps us from achieving the feats we are so capable of? In my opinion, we can narrow down the reasons to:

1.      Fear of Failure
2.      Fear of Success!

If you are afraid, you are in good company. If someone says he/she started their venture without an incessant nudge of fear the person is obviously stretching the truth. It is perfectly natural to be afraid. Fear doesn't come as an alien emotion. It is always there and according to some; fear is what drives us. So instead of symptoms, you have to focus on the cause. Are you not confident in your abilities? Why not check for yourself what you are capable of? If you don't put your skills and talents to challenges how can you label their limits? Have some faith. If you can come up with a wonderful idea as this, surely you are the only one who can make it climb to the sky.

If you didn't set a foot on the journey that is leading towards your goal then how can you be successful? The first step is always the hardest as you have to invest your money, invest your time, overcome your fears and most importantly have faith in yourself.

The first step is the hardest but it is what leads you to the second step and then the third and the fourth and so on.
So what if you fail? Surely, it's still better than to try and to fail than not to ever try at all? Is it not better to try, fail, try again, even fail again; than to have an idea in your head which COULD just be the very next BIG THING, which never materializes because you were fearful of taking the first step, or a number of times I've been to conference and heard *"You know that X…I was going to design that"* my response is never the most polite or considerate *"Really…well, why didn't you*?"

There is a very simple rule in successful business owner's minds if you're going to fail, fail fast! Failing is as important as winning; you see without failing, we don't understand WHAT is it we need to do to succeed! And it's only through failure that we learn to pick ourselves up, dust ourselves off and examine WHY did it fail, in order, we can make the necessary adjustments to go again! Did Thomas Edison try to invest the electric filament light bulb, not get it right first time and say "Ah well, candles are not so bad!?" And there are countless others who in-front of the camera's and the audience will talk about how they have set up from scratch eight separate £Million+ businesses and people think *"WOW"* however how many of them were successful? Creating a £Million+ business is one thing, maintaining that is another, and if it costs £1.1Million to create the £Million turnover then that's not a business it's a nightmare!

Yes, you have to be willing to embrace it. But on the top of all failure is not as bad as it sounds. It can help you ascertain your priorities; it will help you find out the flaws in your plan or execution. You learn a lot once you have taken that leap of faith.

It doesn't matter whether you succeed or are a little unfortunate you will find yourself to be in a better place either way and ready to learn and move on!

It doesn't really matter whether you are in business or not, whether you inherited your parents multi-million-pound empire or have just quit a job, all business owners have a goal, an idea of what success looks like and what the business is going to be able to do in the future; and that's GREAT.

However, life doesn't always pan out that way, in fact; for at least 80% of business owner's life doesn't pan out that way at all! You see 80% of business owners are wrong about EVERYTHING!

I can say this with some certainty. You see, in every sector and every industry business can be categories into one of 5 categories!

There are 1% of businesses in your sector, your industry that is super successful, smashing all the goals and targets and making an obscene amount of money year on year, and there are a further 4% of businesses that are doing very well for themselves, well on the way to joining the '1% club' and just need to trust in the systems and processes they have now created, press the SUPER BOOST accelerator and watch as their business escalates rapidly from doing good to doing GREAT!

There are a further 15% of businesses that are doing OK, growing more traditionally and progressing more slowly year on year.

But in every sector and every industry there are approximately 60% of businesses that are 'getting by' and a further 20% that are FAILING!

These statistics make for very sombre reading, that only 20% of business owners ever even come close to realizing their dream of a successful, expanding and sustainable business, and that 80% of businesses are either 'getting by' or failing! You see, whilst some may have studied business at school, college, university, whilst others have had more 'on the job' style learning, we have all learned 'how to play the game' yet so very few are taught how to win!

Perhaps this stems back to our formal education?

Don't get me wrong, I'm not blaming teachers for these statistics of business failure, I don't blame teachers at all, after all, they were also brought up through the same educational system like the one they are now working within, and using the same antiquated methods of teaching conventional education as we have used for over 150 years! It's not the TEACHERS fault at all, but I would ask you to consider the educational system!

When I attended school, the common mantra throughout my education was: "*Get you head into your books, work hard, study hard, apply yourself and you should then achieve some good grades, which might then result in gaining good employment and if you continue to apply the study hard / work hard philosophy you might then secure a good position and earn good money*" (or something similar) The majority of us, were taught to work hard, apply yourself and your education MIGHT then enable you to achieve good results in life. However, there are more millionaire and billionaires these days that DON'T have an excellent educational background or exam results!

Yet through a new way of working, involving spotting future trends and reacting quickly to maximize exposure to these, through access to the World Wide Web and all that is can enable us to achieve, there are more highly remunerated people who would argue that a formal education was NOT the for most reason they have achieved such wealth, it's more to do with an attitude!

One of my earliest memories of school was standing in the playground huddles around Mr. Phil Strachan. Mr. Strachan was the Physical Education instructor and as such a very popular and admirable figurehead in the school. A group of us were all standing in a semi-circle around Mr. Strachan whilst he was on 'playground' duty, and he posed the inevitable question "What do you want to be when you grow up?" to us all.

The usual answers were heard shouted out eagerly "Footballer, pop star, doctor, astronaut!" I remember even back then at the age of 5 or 6 clearly stating I wanted to own my own business. He stopped and asked why, and I simply said because then I get to choose, what, and where, and when and who! You see it's all about an attitude!

I recently watched with interest a stage show recently where a member of the audience was selected and asked to *"try and move that glass of water"* the audience member, walked to where the glass was placed, picked it up and moved it. However, they were advised they had failed! You see the instruction was TRY and move the water not MOVE the water! There is no effort applied to trying!

Trying does not involve doing (otherwise it would be doing) trying is only willing it to happen, and despite as much WILL as you can muster, nothing will happen, unless you apply DOING!

How many times do we hear *"I'll try harder"* or *"I'm trying to…"* You see one of the biggest identifiers between those in the 1% club and those in the 20% bracket, is whilst those in the 20% bracket are busy telling me WHY it won't work for them and their business, WHY my suggestion or idea has flaws and that it's not relevant, possible or applicable to them and their business!
The 1% club has already implemented it, tested to see if it works and busy building a new sales pipeline to cope with the demand!

You see there are those who say, and those who do, and one of the most fundamental things I've learned in business is to learn to say YES FAST.

It was Richard Branson who is reported to have said *"Even if the idea, suggestion, the opportunity isn't even a complete solution, say YES. Worry about everything else afterward, it's a far better worry to have"* In my continually growing experience, the difference between the 1%, the 4% and the 15% are those not adverse to risk and the speed in which they say YES!

So, before we go any further on this journey together, I want you to spend some time thinking back to DAY 1 of your current business, and I want you to recall your ambition! WHAT did you set out to achieve? What was your goal? Your mission? You Aim? What did success look like back on day 1? What did success MEAN to you then? And has this changed now? If so, WHY has it changed? Have you allowed mediocrity to stem your enthusiasm for that Utopia of true success, or has your idea of success altered?

- Where would you live?
- What size/style of house would it be?
- Would you own one of more than one property?
- Where would you take a holiday?
- How often?
- Where would you children be educated?
- What car would you drive?
- What clothes would you be wearing?
- What else?

You see, those in the 1% club, they have known this right from the very beginning! They set out with such a clear plan of WHAT would success look like, feel like, sound like, smell like, taste like that they have been able to use this as a benchmark to determine if they have remained on the 'right track' towards their goals of super success. And the further down the five-category chart we go, the more we find business owners without a clear vision of what success looks like!

- *"Just bear with me until..."*
- *"It's been a tough year, because..."*
- *"We're in a tough marketplace..."*
- *"That wouldn't work for us because..."*

Believe me; I could write a whole book just on the amount of difference excuses I've heard from lazy and failing business owners who are not willing to accept the simple truth, *"Your business failed because YOU allowed it to happen."*

You might find that an incredibly insensitive and unkind comment, and I can assure you my last intent is to cause any offense. I don't make these comments from anything other than first hand

experience! When one of my business ventures failed, it was ultimately MY FAULT. Sure I could blame a change in legislation, a change in market direction, a change in client requirements, but the fact is, other businesses in my sector (a lot of my competitors) saw this coming and reacted differently to it, and we ultimately failed because we weren't flexible enough to amend our business to cater for requirement. We stuck our heads in the sand and believed the problem would go away, and when it didn't, we got burnt.

**Where there's a will, there's a way**

Many business owners start with a plan that looks something like this:

By the end of year 1, I want to be HERE By the end of year 2, HERE
And by year three we could be HERE!

You see, the 'traditional' way of starting a business including writing a business plan, submitting it to a bank and opening a business account with a line of credit based on the viability of the projections within the plan.

However, I'd like to suggest to you that this is NOT the right way to start a business, it's short-termism and prevents the entrepreneur from understanding the fundamentals of actually starting a business, and nowhere in a business plan does it mention ask or show interest in SUCCESS!

I'd like you to consider for a moment an alternative business plan, one which more and more MODERN Entrepreneurs are using to make oodles of cash quickly and replicate the same plan time and time and time again.

**Before you even begin, determine your exit strategy!**
**...That's right, before you start, determine your end game.**

It was some years ago now when I was invited as a guest of a Business Coach to listen to a multi-millionaire over from Australia on his world tour speaking about Business Success! Of the 2.5Hrs he was on stage, one line resonated with me more than any other:

*"The only true way to measure the success of your business is the day it operates more effectively with you out of it than within it!"*

You see, too many business owners refer to or consider their business as *"my baby."* They see it as 'theirs,' in its infancy they treat it as such, and as it grows likewise, always having an emotional attachment to it and forge their decisions based on those emotions. But the simple fact is this limiting belief is preventing them from actualizing the businesses potential, the fear of success, of it becoming bigger than they ever imagined to the extent that it becomes bigger than them, is preventing them from letting go and allowing it to become so!

My phone is a resource. I use it predominantly for business purposes and if it breaks, or becomes unreliable whilst it has served me well, I will think nothing of trading it in for a newer model.

My car is a resource. I also use it predominantly for business purposes, and just like my phone, whilst I love my car and happy to invest in its upkeep. However, the moment it becomes sluggish, unreliable and costly, it will get replaced.

You MUST start with the end in mind, and this includes seeing and treating your business just as you do your phone and your car.

YOUR BUSINESS IS A RESOURCE! It is used to generate the income, and lifestyle that you (and your employee's desire) YES you need to invest in it, YES you need to keep it well serviced, but to many business owners fail to realize it also needs upgrading, and there may well be a new model on the horizon, that unless you upgrade, your heading for a second-hand dealer and a road to the scrap heap!

As a keynote speaker, I try and keep abreast of modern business thinking and spend considerable time both attending other speaker's events, reading journals, blogs, listening to podcasts and keeping up to date with things.

From this, I find a 'niche' to talk about and regularly write new content to share with my audiences on my observations and research.

I'm not one of those softly, softly speakers who toy with an idea, pose a multiple of possibilities and cajole an audience towards a new consideration. I'm far more bullish in approach, with a controversial title and viewpoint to ignite emotion, debate, to question deep-seated thoughts and beliefs, grab people by the scruff of the neck and pull them from their comfort zone to help them review their position and determine if it remains valid!

My most recent work is entitled 'Is it time to place your child into care?' which already causes either mild humour or more likely great disdain for my viewpoint as it implies you're a failed parent!

However, the title is only being used as a controversial metaphor about the majority of business owners who fail to allow their business to grow, by continually treating it as *"their baby."*

When a child is first born, it is defenceless and requires the love, care, and attention of either parents or guardians to survive. However, as the baby turns, to toddler, child, teenager, and adult the requirements of the parent/guardian change from that of the provider to the facilitator, away from the provision of and more to enabler.

Society would view it as extremely wrong for a parent to continue to treat a toddler, child, teenager, and adult the same as when the baby was first born. As an adult, I would take great offense at someone else trying to feed, bath, dress me, yet when it comes to the growth and development of a small business, there are so many micro-managing every last decision so significantly that it remains in its infancy, never having been allowed to grow and develop!

**Start with the end in mind**

How many times have we heard that before, yet for the majority it appears completely foreign to be thinking about the company's sales value and your exit strategy before you have even begun to trade! This is exactly the right time to be planning what is the PURPOSE of the business. To what PURPOSE does the business need to serve you?

How much money does the business need to generate? Over what period? What time and resource are you prepared to commit to this process? And most importantly are your goals achievable?

I'd like to share with you for a second or two a brief story about a guy I once met call, Ryan. Ryan was in his early 30's had a wife and a young family and already had some business successes under his belt.

One day he launched a website (Let's call it Gunfreeamerica.com) it was a membership site, where for an initial payment of just $17 and then subsequent monthly payments of $7, you got a GUN FREE AMERICA bumper sticker and access to all the content shared on the site about why America should amend its gun laws and become a no firearm country. He published the site, broadcast on all the relevant social media platforms and watched as literally hundreds and hundreds of people flocked to sign up to show their support for a gun free country.

A couple of weeks later another new website was launched (let's call it myrighttobeararms.com) and for an initial payment of $17 and subsequent payments of just $7 a month you could subscribe to receive a bumper sticker and all the content talking about why it's every human's right to protect themselves and their family, why the constitution deems it to be so, and they shall continue to bear arms as part of their human rights.

Guess what, BOTH sites are owned by the same guy – Ryan. You see, Ryan doesn't have that much of an opinion on the gun laws in America, what Ryan DOES HAVE is the ability to see an opportunity to benefit from OTHER PEOPLES opinion. He outsources all the copy for the website each month to a bunch of People who are FOR or AGAINST the subject, and has another team of people responsible for updating the website and drawing traffic to each of the sites. He has seized the opportunity to 'Feed a starving crowd'.  He has identified an opportunity that nobody else had, and commercialized that into a HIGHLY SUCCESSFUL Business. According to Ryan collectively the sites generate over **$5.2M PER MONTH** in revenue, and continue to grow month on month as more and more people from all over the world show their support for one side of the debate or the other!

As Michael Gerber first spoke about within his world best-selling book the E-Myth, too many business owners are technicians within their business. The Chef who got sick of working so many hours in a hot kitchen seeing how much they got paid compared to how much each dish is sold for and decided to become a restaurant owner! Or the mechanic who got sick of working so many hours under the bonnet of a vehicle saw their pay against
the 'labour' fee on the invoice to the client and chose to set up their garage. It's NOT necessarily about doing what YOUR good at that counts, it's all about identifying a market that is hungry for something you could provide in a better, cleaner, faster, safer, more exciting, more interesting manner than anyone else, it's about identifying a gap in the market and filling that space.

So, go back to the dream, your dream NOT a dream of owning a colossal business that operates all over the globe, has tons of staff and buildings and stuff, but about your LIFE GOALS!

What is YOUR PURPOSE? What do YOU want to achieve in life? What do you want to be remembered for? Where do you want to be, do, have? It's only once you have clearly identified these things, that we can even begin to formulate a business that's going to be congruent with your goals to enable you to achieve them, ANYTHING else is simply a distraction, tearing you away from what YOU want to achieve!

## Chapter 2 - Goal Setting

Most of us recognize that to get anything achieved we really ought to have a plan. It doesn't matter whether your four years old and learning how to tie your shoe laces or 40 years old and running a shoe manufacturing business, to prevent chaos we achieve goals by having a plan.

However, the traditional method of achieving these goals is fundamentally flawed because we are human! Our natural inquisitive state prevents us from following the traditional methods of goal setting and goal achievement, yet we still carry on and use these methods! (And that's BONKERS)

As alluded to in the first chapter I want you to have identified WHAT YOU want to achieve IN LIFE! It's only then we can determine WHAT do we need to do to realize those life long goals.

It was Jim Rohan that once said, "The most important benefit of setting goals isn't achieving your goal; it's what you do and the person you become to achieve your goal that's the real benefit."

Goal setting is powerful because it provides focus. It shapes our dreams. It gives us the ability to hone in on the exact actions we need to perform to achieve everything we desire in life. Goals are great because they cause us to stretch and grow in ways that we never have before. To reach our goals, we must become better.

Life is designed in such a way that we look long-term and live short-term. We dream of the future and live in the present. Unfortunately, the present can produce many challenging obstacles. But setting goals provides long-term vision in our lives. We all need powerful, long-range goals to help us get past those short- term obstacles. Fortunately, the more powerful our goals are, the more we'll be able to act on and guarantee that they will come to pass.

Many people feel as if they're adrift in the world. They work hard, but they don't seem to get anywhere worthwhile.

A key reason that they feel this way is that they haven't spent enough time thinking about what they want from life, and haven't set themselves formal goals.

After all, would you set out on a major journey with no real idea of your destination? Probably not!

Goal setting is a powerful process for thinking about your ideal future, and for motivating yourself to turn your vision of this future into reality.

The process of setting goals helps you choose where you want to go in life. By knowing precisely what you want to achieve, you know where you have to concentrate your efforts. You'll also quickly spot the distractions that can, so easily, lead you astray.

**Why Set Goals?**

Top-level athletes, successful business-people and achievers in all fields all set goals. Setting goals gives you long-term vision and short-term motivation. It focuses your acquisition of knowledge and helps you to organize your time and your resources so that you can make the very most of your life.

By setting sharp, clearly defined goals, you can measure and take pride in the achievement of those goals, and you'll see forward progress in what might previously have seemed a long pointless grind. You will also raise your self-confidence, as you recognize your ability and competence in achieving the goals that you've set.

I certainly remember well the first time I sat with my wife and discussed my goals for my career as a Combat Medic Technician within the British Army. You see, there are two primary methods in which to achieve promotion within the Medical Corps. Firstly, (and most popular) is to be a good enough medic but an exceptional soldier!

After all, you're in the Army, you're working alongside infantry and other front line troops, and you all consider 'soldier first, career second' so to be an exceptional soldier is both the best way of staying alive and getting recognised as an ASSET to the regiment.
The second, (and ironically less popular method) was to be a good enough soldier and an exceptional medic! To do enough not to be a danger or hindrance to either your section, platoon or section, but to be so qualified, experienced and capable as a medic that the team WANTED to have you there, because when the S**t hit the fan, they knew they were in the best of hands and more likely to get out of it at the other end!

I opted quite clearly and quite early on in my military career to be the later rather than the former! Whilst I understood the importance of fitness, combat readiness and the ability to 'dig in' when needed, my efforts, interests and goals were to be the very best medic I could be, and hope that was sufficient to be recognised and promoted accordingly (as and when the time and opportunity arose)

**Starting to Set Personal Goals**

You set your goals on some levels:

•      **First**, you create your "big picture" of what you want to do with your life (or over, say, the next ten years), and identify the large-scale goals that you want to achieve.

- **Then**, you break these down into the smaller and smaller targets that you must hit to reach your lifetime goals.

- **Finally**, once you have your plan, you start working on it to achieve these goals.

This is why we start the process of setting goals by looking at your lifetime goals. Then, we work down on the things that you can do in, say, the next five years, then next year, next month, next week, and today, to start moving towards them.

## Step 1: Setting Lifetime Goals

The first step in setting personal goals is to consider what you want to achieve in your lifetime (or at least, by a significant and distant age in the future). Setting lifetime goals gives you the overall perspective that shapes all other aspects of your decision- making.

To give a broad, balanced coverage of all important areas in your life, try to set goals in some of the following categories (or in other categories of your own, where these are important to you):

- **Career** – What level do you want to reach in your career, or what do you want to achieve?

- **Financial** – How much do you want to earn, by what stage? How is this related to your career goals?

- **Education** – Is there any knowledge you want to acquire in particular? What information and skills will you need to have to achieve other goals?

- **Family** – Do you want to be a parent? If so, how are you going to be a good parent? How do you want to be seen by a partner or by members of your extended family?

- **Artistic** – Do you want to achieve any artistic goals?

- **Attitude** – Is any part of your mind-set holding you back? Is there any part of the way that you behave that upsets you? (If so, set a goal to improve your behaviour or find a solution to the problem.)

- **Physical** – Are there any athletic goals that you want to achieve, or do you want good health deep into old age? What steps are you going to take to achieve this?

- **Pleasure** – How do you want to enjoy yourself? (You should ensure that some of your life is for you!)

- **Public Service** – Do you want to make the world a better place? If so, how?

Spend some time brainstorming these things, and then select one or more goals in each category that best reflect what you want to do. Then consider trimming again so that you have a small number of really significant goals that you can focus on.

As you do this, make sure that the goals that you have set are ones that you genuinely want to achieve, not ones that your parents, family, or employers might want. (If you have a partner, you probably want to consider what he or she wants – however, make sure that you also remain true to yourself!)

**Step 2: Setting Smaller Goals**

Once you have set your lifetime goals, set a five-year plan of smaller goals that you need to complete if you are to reach your lifetime plan.

Then create a one-year plan, six-month plan, and a one-month plan of progressively smaller goals that you should reach to achieve your lifetime goals. Each of these should be based on the previous plan.

Then create a daily To-Do List of things that you should do today to work towards your lifetime goals.

At an early stage, your smaller goals might be to read books and gather information on the achievement of your higher-level goals. This will help you to improve the quality and realism of your goal setting.

Finally, review your plans, and make sure that they fit the way in which you want to live your life.

**Staying on Course**

Once you've decided on your first set of goals, keep the process going by reviewing and updating your To-Do List on a daily basis.

Periodically review the longer-term plans, and modify them to reflect your changing priorities and experience. (A good way of doing this is to schedule regular, repeating reviews using a computer-based diary.)

**SMART Goals**

I know we first spoke about the benefits and importance of SMART goals in my first book 'Battlefield2Boardroom – 10 Proven Military Strategies to Combat Mediocrity[1]' However, for those yet to purchase a copy! A useful way of making goals more powerful is to use the SMART mnemonic. While there are plenty of variants SMART usually stands for:

- S – Specific (or Significant).

- M – Measurable (or Meaningful).

- A – Attainable (or Action-Oriented).

- R – Relevant (or Rewarding).

- T – Time-bound (or Trackable).

For example, instead of having "*to visit the North Pole*" as a goal, it's more powerful to use the SMART goal "*To have completed my trip trekking to the North Pole by 31 December 2017.*" Obviously, this will only be attainable if a lot of preparation has been completed beforehand!

---

[1] Further details about this book, and to purchase your signed copy: Visit www.Battlefield2Boardroom.co.uk

**Let me offer you an example, by sharing MY life goal...**

I'd like to live on a 3-4 acre plot of land in South West France. It will have a main 6-bedroom house with beautiful views over the estate and down towards the coast, with a couple of outbuildings stemming from it and 4 x 3 bedroom gites. There will be two pools (one for the main house occupants, and another shared for the occupants of the gites) The first of the outbuildings shall consist of a garage on the ground floor, and a boardroom and office, with a veranda on the first floor! The other outbuilding shall be composed of a self-contained flat on the upper floor and a recording studio on the ground floor! A third building which separates the main house from the gites shall consist of a gymnasium in the basement and a commercial kitchen on the ground floor!

My intention is, that in the summer months, I'll commercially let the gites as holiday lets, and during the winter months, invite an unsigned band to make use of the recording studio (rather than simple record in a city centre somewhere back home) with the availability to shoot a promo video in southern France! The self-contained flat shall be used to invite a music student to take residence 'gap year option' or 'sabbatical' with free use of flat and studio in exchange for being willing to welcome gite guests and provide entertainment at the weekend! The kitchen could be used to offer B&B, half board or even full board if we chose! And the gym, other than a little self-indulgence, perhaps others also see the benefit that a healthy body leads to a healthy mind?

I'll always want an office to hide away in (can't see myself ever 'retiring' as I love what I do) and the boardroom will enable me that one weekend a month, I invite business owners to join me in France for Mastermind. The gites are sufficient in number to manage a mastermind group, the boardroom (and the veranda) ample space for the mastermind and the commercial kitchen can be opened up with a hired a chef to cater for them whilst they are on site.

The main house is positioned carefully enough NOT to be distracted by any commercial activities going on, and as such enables me to have a great work/life balance, and the business to fund my lifestyle most effectively.

I've got the plans, I know where I want to build it, I've done all the numbers, I have a CLEAR GOAL, and I'm working every day towards fulfilling that goal with the actions I take. It's clear, I'm not going to deviate from it, I have a proposed date of execution, and IT'S REAL.

**Further Tips for Setting Your Goals**

•        State each goal as a positive statement – Express your goals positively – "Execute this technique well" is a much better goal than "Don't make this stupid mistake."

•        Be precise: Set precise goals, putting in dates, times and amounts so that you can measure achievement. If you do this, you'll know exactly when you have achieved the goal, and can take complete satisfaction from having achieved it.

•        Set priorities – When you have several goals, give each priority. This helps you to avoid feeling overwhelmed by having too many goals and helps to direct your attention to the most important ones.

•        Write goals down – This crystallizes them and gives them more force.

•        Keep operational goals small – Keep the low-level goals that you're working towards small and achievable. If a goal is too large, then it can seem that you are not making progress towards it. Keeping goals small and incremental gives more opportunities for reward.

•        Set performance goals, not outcome goals – You should take care to set goals over which you have as much control as possible. It can be quite dispiriting to fail to achieve a personal goal for reasons beyond your control!

In business, these reasons could be bad business environments or unexpected effects of government policy. In sport, they could include poor judging, bad weather, injury, or just plain bad luck.

If you base your goals on personal performance, then you can keep control over the achievement of your goals, and draw satisfaction from them.

- Set realistic goals – It's important to set goals that you can achieve. All sorts of people (for example, employers, parents, media, or society) can set unrealistic goals for you. They will often do this in ignorance of your desires and ambitions.

It's also possible to set goals that are too difficult because you might not appreciate either the obstacles in the way or understand quite how much skill you need to develop to achieve a particular level of performance.

## Achieving Goals

When you've achieved a goal, take the time to enjoy the satisfaction of having done so. Absorb the implications of the goal achievement, and observe the progress that you've made towards other goals.

If the goal was a significant one, reward yourself appropriately. All of this helps you build the self-confidence you deserve.

With the experience of having achieved this goal, review the rest of your goal plans:

- If you achieved the goal too easily, make your next goal harder.

- If the goal took a dispiriting length of time to achieve, make the next goal a little easier.

- If you learned something that would lead you to change other goals, do so.

- If you noticed a deficit in your skills despite achieving the goal, decide whether to set goals to fix this.

Feed lessons you have learned back into the process of setting your next goals. Remember too that your goals will change as time goes on.

Adjust them regularly to reflect growth in your knowledge and experience, and if goals do not hold any attraction any longer, consider letting them go.

**The key aspects to learn and remember when goal setting:**

1.      Evaluate and reflect.

The only way we can reasonably decide what we want in the future and how we'll get there is to know where we are right now and what our current level of satisfaction is. So first, take some time to think through and write down your current situation; then ask this question on each key point: Is that OK?

The purpose of evaluation is twofold. First, it gives you an objective way to look at your accomplishments and your pursuit of the vision you have for life. Secondly, it shows you where you are so you can determine where you need to go. Evaluation gives you a baseline to work from.

Take a couple of hours this week to evaluate and reflect. See where you are and write it down so that as the month's progress and you continue a regular time of evaluation and reflection, you will see just how much ground you're gaining—and that will be exciting!

2.      Define your dreams and goals.

One of the amazing things we have been given as humans is the unquenchable desire to have dreams of a better life and the ability to establish and set goals to live out those dreams. We can look deep within our hearts and dream of a better situation for our families and ourselves. We can dream of better financial, emotional, spiritual or physical lives. We have also been given the ability to not only dream, but also pursue those dreams—and not just pursue them, but the cognitive ability to lay out a plan and strategies to achieve those dreams.

What are your dreams and goals? This isn't what you already have or what you have done, but what you want. Have you ever really sat down and thought through your life values and decided what you want? Have you ever taken the time to reflect truly, to listen quietly to your heart, to see what dreams live within you? Your dreams are there. Everyone has them. They may live right on the surface, or they may be buried deep from years of others telling you they were foolish, but they are there.

Take time to be quiet. This is something that we don't do enough of in this busy world of ours. We rush; rush, rush, and we're constantly listening to noise all around us. The human heart was meant for times of quiet—to peer deep within. It is when we do this that our hearts are set free to soar and take flight on the wings of our dreams. Schedule some quiet "dream time" this week. No other people. No cell phone. No computer. Just you, a pad, a pen and your thoughts.

Think about what thrills you. When you are quiet, think about those things that get your blood moving. What would you love to do, either for fun or a living? What would you love to accomplish?

What would you try if you were guaranteed to succeed? What big thoughts move your heart into a state of excitement and joy?
When you answer these questions, you will feel great, and you will be in the "dream zone." It is only when we get to this point that we experience what our dreams are.

Write down all of your dreams as you have them. Don't think of any as too outlandish or foolish—remember—you're dreaming! Let the thoughts fly and take the careful record.

Now, prioritize those dreams. Which are most important? Which are most feasible? Which would you love to do the most? Put them in the order in which you will try to attain them.
Remember, we are always moving toward action—not just dreaming.

3.      Make your goals S.M.A.R.T.

Goals are no place to waffle. They are no place to be vague. Ambiguous goals produce ambiguous results. Incomplete goals produce incomplete futures.

Always set goals that are measurable. I would say "specifically measurable" to take into account our principle of being specific.

One of the detrimental things that many people do—with good intentions is setting goals that are so high that they are unattainable.

The root word of realistic is "real." A goal has to be something that we can reasonably make "real" or a "reality" in our lives. Some goals are simply not realistic. You have to be able to say, even if it is a tremendously stretching goal, that yes, indeed, it is entirely realistic—that you could make it. You may even have to say that it will take x, y and z to do it, but if those happen, then it can be done. This is in no way to say it shouldn't be a big goal, but it must be realistic.

Every goal should have a timeframe attached to it. One of the powerful aspects of a great goal is that it has an end—a time in which you are shooting to accomplish it.
As time goes by, you work on it because you don't want to get behind, and you work diligently because you want to meet the deadline. You may even have to break down a big goal into different parts of measurement and timeframes—that is OK. Set smaller goals and work them out in their own time. A S.M.A.R.T. goal has a timeline.

4.      Have accountability.

When someone knows what your goals are, they hold you accountable by asking you to "give an account" of where you are in the process of achieving that goal. Accountability puts some teeth into the process. If a goal is set and only one person knows it, does it have any power? Many times, no. A goal isn't as powerful if you don't have one or more people who can hold you accountable to it.

Imagination and motivation are powerful things, and with them on your side, you have all the reason in the world to achieve your grandest dreams. Need proof?...

Take the story of how the first bridge over the Niagara River near Niagara Falls was built in 1847...

To build a bridge over the giant gorge, the builders first had to get a line over the canyon, from one side to the other— from the United States to Canada with roaring rapids underneath. Except the engineers couldn't cross the river in a boat because it would go over the falls, the airplane hadn't been invented yet, and the distance was way beyond bow-and-arrow range.

The designing engineer, Charles Ellet, pondered the dilemma until he came up with a revolutionary idea: to sponsor a kite-flying contest. A $5 prize (a small lottery back then!) would go to the person who could fly a kite across the gorge and let it go low enough to the ground for someone on the other side to grab the

string. It was successful—a young American boy won the contest on his second attempt.

The kite string, fastened to a tree, was used to pull a cord across, then a line, then a rope. Next came an iron-wire cable and then steel cables, until a structure strong enough to build a suspension bridge was in place. The bridge opened on 1st August 1848. And it all began with an idea and one thin kite string.

That string is like a single thought. The more vivid and clear the thought, and the more you come back to it, the stronger it becomes—like the string to the rope to the cable. Each time you rethink it, dwell on it or layer it with other thoughts, you are strengthening the structure on which to build your idea, like building a bridge over Niagara Falls.

But unlike a kite, there is no string attached to how high and how far your goals may take you. They are limited only by the power of your imagination and the strength of your desire.

Before you read any further, just STOP and consider what you want to achieve, not in business BUT LIFE, go on; I dare you to DREAM...

## Chapter 3 - Team Selection

*"If we want to go fast, go alone,*
*If we want to go far, go as a team."*

I know I also used this African proverb at the start of the TEAM chapter within my first book (Battlefield2Boardroom – 10 Military Strategies to Combat Business Mediocrity) however it's as relevant here as is there, and we'll be reviewing TEAM rather differently here!

I remember standing in line with all the other kids waiting for my turn to 'get picked' to join either the blue team or the red team for that infamous game of street football! The two best football players on the street had already deemed THEY were to be team captains, and a surge of chests were puffed up as those eager to play for one side or the other, stood on their tiptoes with bated breath desperate to be considered their 'number 2' or number 3, or 4 or 5!

I knew I wasn't that good at football; it wasn't my thing. When everyone else had first begun kicking a football around, I was at home learning to play the piano! And with a father who wasn't at all interested in sport, and no older brother to admire, it just had never become my thing. I knew I was there to keep the numbers up and wasn't even trusted to stand in goal, so would become a reluctant pick for either team and be given the job of a defender!

It was just the same later on in life when I was a lot older and in work, only this time although not a 'team captain' I was picked as 'number 2'. This time it was a long-range orienteering competition with tasks to complete along the way and always against the clock on a time trial. All the way through my basic training in the British Army, I'd proven to be very good at getting my bearings, understanding my way around a compass and always made quick progress, in this 'sport' I wasn't last.

The point I'm trying to make here is, your utopia is not a popularity contest, and as such your team, those people around you, encouraging you, guiding you shouldn't be picked on any other basis than being the very best at what they do (possibly even better than you) and be absolutely determined to ensure YOU achieve everything YOU set out to do.

I'd like to share with you an exceedingly brief look at Scott's most ill-fated goal to be the first the reach the Pole. There are a variety of widely speculative versions of events regarding WHAT was the cause of such a tragic end to the endeavour, and my reflection of this, is not to add to this speculation; however, there were a number of fundamental principles that were to be the tell-tale signs of a disastrous end to the quest well before the final resting place of Scott and his team were confirmed.

Scott had been born into a family with a mixed background spanning some generations of either Army or Naval service and so was no surprise he chose to follow this path of employment.

Whilst his father had been both a magistrate and 'brewer' and Scott had benefited from a certain degree of wealth and comfort whilst he was a child and able to attend school and naval training early in life (as did his brother) and joined the Navy at just 13.

Scott was a hard working young man, with a clear plan for what he wanted to achieve, and steadily worked his way through rank and opportunity throughout his early military career. However, back home in Plymouth his father had sold the brewery business, invested the money unwisely and the news got to Scott that the family was close to bankruptcy, his father now old and in ill health.

There was a sudden urgency for him to increase his income drastically, and for this, he would need to find a way of significantly speeding up his promotions substantially.

A chance meeting whilst on leave in London with Sir Clements Markham, president of the Royal Geographical Society where he learned of the impending 'Discovery' expedition to Antarctica, and he realized this was his only sure way of escalating his opportunity of promotional sufficiently to afford his new added family financial commitments.

Although Sir Clements was taken by Scott, the board of the Royal Geographical Society were less so, suggesting in favour of a far more experienced naval leader and crew with a scientist to lead the expedition, not a relatively junior naval commander.

However, Sire Clements had made his decision and Scott was to lead the expedition.

However, Scott was not the only one wishing to take this crown. His old friend and colleague Ernest Shackleton were also on a quest to be crowned first to the South Pole, and this race to the Pole would cost Scott dearly at the end in regards to loyalty, support, and clarity of communication.

Whilst I don't want to detract from this book by spending too long looking at the downfall of Scott. The point I wish you to stop and consider is, there were some other factors that whilst not DIRECTLY responsible for Scott failing to be crowned the first, or in the fate of his trip back, these were all significant indirect contributory factors to his overall failure and subsequent death.

There are many who have 'risked it all' and lost not only THEIR EVERYTHING but that of family, friends, colleagues and loved ones in their shared support and belief in the goals and aspirations of a few. But what I do want, no; NEED you to understand is there is the countless manner of ways in which we can get blown off course along the way, be it directly through 'Shiny Object Syndrome' or more indirectly by the infinite number of other factors which may challenge our resolve.

If we are to have ANY chance of actually achieving UTOPIA (rather than simply 'something more than we have already'), we must understand 1. The resolve WE must have in achieving it and 2.
That EVERYONE on our team is the same absolute resolve as we are that THIS is the goal and nothing shall prevent us from achieving it.

I'm reminded here of the very famous Will Smith quote regarding success and the Treadmill! If you're not aware of it? I certainly recommend you look it up, alternatively simply follow this link to listen to him explain!

As a medic in the army, you are often 'loaned' to whichever regiment requires a medic with your skills, qualifications, rank and experience dependent on the nature of the deployment and perceived need. I remember most fondly the short amount of time I spent working alongside 'The Black Watch.'

In any Highland regiment, every individual feels that his conduct is the subject of observation that, independently of his duty, as a member of a systematic whole he has a separate and individual reputation to sustain, which will be reflected on his family, on his family and district or Glen"
The words above are as relevant today as they were when first written by the 19th century Black Watch historian. They continue that the 'Black Watch' boasts a history of honour, gallantry and devoted service to both Kings and Queens and country. The battles which have contributed most significantly to these claims have been the ones in which the odds have been most formidable.  From Fontenoy to Fallujah with Waterloo, Alamein and 2 world wars in between, the Black Watch have played a significant part in each of these bloody and mighty conflicts, and the sheer scope and scale of the Black Watch's contribution are what has continued to nurture a deep pride in this great regiment, way beyond the modern day rules and regulations of today's army.

A team willing to die for its cause, a team who understand that it is far greater collectively than any one man alone, is a team that makes things happen!

I'd like to share with you a little information about the team here at My TrueNORTH.....

No-one has a job description!
No-one has a designated job title!
No-one has specific Terms and Conditions of employment!

What we DO have is a set of Attitudes and Behaviours which we ALL subscribe to! Let me explain.....

> **"If we always do, what we've always done;**
> **We'll always have, what we've already got"**

If I wanted a set of people who perform the same as everyone else does as an employee working to help someone else get closer and closer to THEIR utopia, then I'd probably recruit in the same manner as everyone else, hire in the same way as everyone else, and have similar terms of work.......AS EVERYONE ELSE!

But I don't want a life as anyone else, my Utopia is unique to me and not like anything else, so why would I ever constrain my thinking to attract others JUST LIKE EVERYONE ELSE?

We don't have scheduled times of work! We don't have scheduled days of work, we don't even have a designated Christmas break policy (all those reading this with any sort of HR background are probably quaking in their boots right now) but the fact is; if I want to attract a team of forward thinking, proactive and ethical leaders, whether they are managing my marketing and social media, my sales and negotiation, my personal and professional development, even my finances and 'the numbers'.

If I truly want to be ethical and attract those who subscribe to my view of utopia, why on earth would I retrain their thinking or proactive thinking with such things as rules and regulations, timings and personal performance indicators why would I in one breath say, *"I need you to buy into this ethical belief that collectively we can create this vision I happen to call utopia"*, and in the next breath say *"Oh, by the way, I'm docking 15mins pay because you are late!"*

I need you to have freedom of vision and expression, but can you do it for me 40hrs a week between 8 am and 5 pm five days a week, please?

I need you to commit YOUR future to achieving a shared vision of utopia, but I'll have to discipline you if you don't do it my way!

REALLY?

Are we a team of explorers seeking to break boundaries and ready to commit EVERYTHING to a shared understanding of what that is, or are we a team of business coaches seeking to make a huge profit and take lots of exotic holidays?

The African proverb I opened this chapter with is simply SO TRUE. If you want to make money quick, don't let me or reading anymore stop you from creating a pop-up shop, a landing and squeeze page or whatever else it is you are so compelled to do to make a few quid overnight!

But, if your wanting to be ground-breaking, to challenge beliefs, to rock the world and leave a legacy long after you've gone as *"The person who…"* then you have to start way before you set out by carefully sourcing a team that buys into the belief as much as you, and are as committed to its success as you are.

**REMEMBER**: Qualifications can be earned, experienced can be gained but attitude must come from within! Pick people with the right attitude, values, ethics, and morals, and you've got a team that will collectively take you far beyond your wildest dreams!

Pick unwisely, and you'll be on life's Helter skelter for a LONG time to come!

Just as you've begun to accept the absurdity of this concept, I'm going to throw you another. 97.5% of people will not stay in the same job throughout their life, so WHY do we get upset, frustrated, angry even when someone approaches us and says, "sincerest of thanks, but I'd like to tender my resignation."

Ironically whilst writing this chapter, I've received notification from one of the back office staff within my coaching business: My TrueNORTH Ethical Coaching, that she is tendering her resignation today! She's been with the company for the past 18 months now, and having learned lots about who we are and what we do, has deemed she'd like to leave employment to form her own business! She shall leave in the next few weeks with our blessing and best wishes to launch as a solopreneur! (The cost of encouraging entrepreneurship right there!)

I've shared with you in the last few pages, MY idea of utopia. My French Chateau with surrounding Gites, commercial kitchen, gym, boardroom and music studio! My utopia.

Yes, I've got an idea I'm likely to be sharing this with others, but nowhere in my plan is my accountant, marketing manager, head of sales and HR director living on site in the gites!

**ALL EMPLOYMENT IS TRANSIENT!**

Recent studies have suggested that less than 1.5% of the working population within the Western world shall enter employment, and stick to that one role until they retire. A Job for life is almost a thing of the past, yet so many business owners get frustrated and disappointed, angry even when a member of 'their team' sets sail on a different journey!

I acknowledge, we are most likely to achieve our utopia quicker and easier with a team to help, support, guide and collectively move forward. But unless your utopia is a commune, then once you've 'got there' your unlikely to have need of the team who helped you achieve it!

Finally, on this point, I'd like to share with you a brief story about my good friend Adam of which some of you will know WHO I am referring.

Adam had a good friend in school with whom they often set each other challenges. Who could do this first, the fastest, the best, the smartest, they were competitive kids challenging each other to achieve.

- For some reason, I said I would be a millionaire when I was older, one of them said the newspaper recently said that a million pound is no longer enough to have a millionaire lifestyle. So I said, I'll make £10m then. Then one said, but when we're older, that figure will have changed again. So I said, £50 F***in' million by the time I'm 35 then!!!!

No one else really took on the challenge. Every job I took was based on "*would I learn something to get me closer.*" I have made so many decisions, which on paper don't make sense, but in the context of £50m it does. Like quitting my well-paid job with a kid on the way to start a training company at the start of a recession! I set up another business, which made £1m in the first 18 months, but it wasn't scalable beyond that. So I walked away. I launched other things, which had the potential, but it wasn't until taking on a team of high calibre people that things started to fall into place. Right model, right market, feed a starving affluent crowd, etc.

In truth, I don't see it as £50m turnover. I see it as a £50m net worth. If we make a £5m profit and I've specifically worked on a model that tends to get 10x bit on exit, then I'll claim to have hit the goal.

In the context of this book, yes, my true north does change. Having kids, the market, my health, etc., it all changes my desire, my considerations, my appetite.

My big wake-up call is... nearly everyone says they're WHY, their purpose is "*the health and happiness of their family and kids*" etc. But I think that's BS. I think everyone has that. Employed people have that. I think to achieve something bigger than yourself you need a goal, which is slightly irrational and unique to you. For me, £50M underpins it. Of course, I do it for my family, but that goes without saying. Or maybe I do, do it for me, so what. Like Gary Vee with buying the Jets. He doesn't want to buy the Jets; it's the pursuit of buying the jets that drive him.

Would I have achieved this without a mentor, in fact over the time a whole series of mentors, guides, coaches (call them what you will) defiantly not, I wouldn't have even considered half the things had I not had a team of people in my corner, encouraging me to keep thinking big, but once you have the right team, the right mentor, the right attitude, anything in the world becomes possible!"

I first met Adam in his late 20's. He was Managing Director of 2 companies and about to become a millionaire! But £50M was still a long way off, and I remember him telling me this story and how he would have to rethink his business growth strategy if he had a shot of going for the £50M goal he'd originally agreed to!

I've followed Adam closely over the past 18 months as he's shared almost daily with a group of around 16 of us, his journey to £50M the decision making, sacrifices, mind-set changes he's had to make in order to recalibrate his time, his thoughts, his efforts in order to go from £1M to £2M, from £2M to £5M and how this thinking has shaped his decisions, his outlook, the focus and considerations he's made along the way to accelerate the growth sufficiently to be 'on track' for the £50M turnover by 2020!

Then at the beginning of September 2016 came the bombshell! Adam revealed to us (as 16 supporters, accountability partners, independent witnesses, call us what you will) that he felt dismayed to reveal the board of the business had sat, and determined they planned to prepare the business for sale in early 2017 hoping to raise between £10M-£12M!

Don't get me wrong; this business has gone from start-up to a potential £12M sell out in approximately three years! Which in itself is an incredible achievement and one, which many others would deem a resounding success!

But rather than be excited the potential of selling a three-year-old business for £12M this news has come as a shock and disappointment as Adam feels the chance to hit his original £50M goal may have become less realistic than more!

**There are two stark lessons to learn here:**

1.      YOUR Utopia IS NOT theirs!
As mentioned within this chapter, nowhere in my South of France estate is there an allocation for my current team to live and share with me MY GOALS. Employment is Transient, and those who get you to where you are right now, are most likely NOT to be the ones who help you achieve your final goals!

2.      With this in mind, Adam has two choices

a.      Either accept the £12M sell out and say "it's not bad to have achieved this before I'm 35Years old!"

b.      Or, accept the buyout, and use the funds to sink into another project with the knowledge, wisdom, and determination to grow from £12M to £25M and possibly then from £25M to £100M

It's about understanding not to hang our hat on ONE hope, but to understand how to adapt our plans, aspirations, dreams, goals from one opportunity to another quickly and without losing sight on WHAT IS IT ALL FOR...

UNLESS, we come to accept the absolute, that utopia is part of the journey, and we never really get to one final designated place, and that just like the North and South pole, just like Adam alluded to in regards to him becoming a husband, father, etc. Success continues to move also, whereas 'Utopia' is perhaps a state of mind, rather than a physical place, or time or wealth. Perhaps Utopia is actually at one with who we are, where we are when we are and happy to continually strive to be and remain the very best version of you that you can be along life's journey!

## Chapter 4 - The Right Equipment

Whilst many people starting out in business have this idea that to start out in business we need the latest phone, the latest laptop, a new functional branded vehicle, an all singing all dancing swanky new website, email address and business cards...

I'm going to suggest to you that whilst all of that MAY be necessary for your chosen business, the RIGHT equipment is a calculator, a pen and paper and a watch! (Or for those techie people, otherwise known as a spreadsheet!)

**Start by asking yourself these two sets of questions:**

1. What am I particularly good at, that others might want/need and that if I don't do (or do it my way) might well not get done?

OR...

1. Are there sufficient people who require this to warrant me doing it?
2. How much of that market do I require to achieve My Utopia?
3. What is my exit strategy once I have achieved it?

## Why OR?

The first question is about YOU, YOUR ability, talent, capability whatever you want to call it or label it as, but it's about what is going to be YOUR contribution to the world?

The second questions are about the world and about whether what you have to offer is what the world wants!

For example:

I know of a young lady is exceptionally talented at crochet! Without use of a design or plan, she can make incredible designs both 2 and 3 dimensional from table decorations to clothing and from artistic to very practical (Her full sized koala bear is quite amazing!)

HOWEVER, unfortunately for her, the world is not screaming out for crochet Koala bears! And so her business model is somewhat flawed if she was hoping to retire off either teaching everyone else or from Koala bear sales!

In another example, I know of 2 ladies who have been working for YEARS on developing a serum as an alternative to the use of Botox within aesthetic medicine!

Well over 15Million procedures are carried out PER YEAR, with an average length of time between each procedure of just four months and no sign of the industry growth slowing, a competitor to Botox is likely to make overnight multi-millionaires of whoever finds a suitable alternative.

However, aside from the money, the morals and everything in- between I want you to consider your LIFE and determine HOW you want to fill it?

If having the freedom to sit happily and crochet Koala's is life fulfilling for you, and the thought of being flown all over the world for press interviews, running clinics on the four corners of the globe and having demand for your product outstrip ability to produce it frightens the life out of you, then perhaps the first question is sufficient.

Whereas if you want to 'make a difference' if your plan of utopia does include a legacy then perhaps it might be far better to start with the end in mind (just like Adam) and determine WHAT you need to do, in WHAT time frame for dreams to become a reality?

This chapter is all about the tools for the job, though, so there is also need to understand we don't need to re- invent the wheel these days.

A friend of mine and fellow international speaker Michael Jackson speaks eloquently and inspiringly about the Speed of Change, and that within one lifetime we are already 10's if not 100's of times faster than we were!

If we are going to SCALE our business, we must start by considering WHAT RESOURCES do I have, do I need, and are they available for me to spend less time achieving more. More value, more opportunity, more reach, more opportunity, more revenue.

In Michael's exceptional example, within one lifetime, we've gone from Drafting, Writing, sending a letter and awaiting a reply by the same means, to predictive text, whereby a computer determines WHAT your likely to say before you have even said it!

So my question for you in regards to Utopia, is not what do you want to achieve within your lifetime, but what are you going to achieve in the next 12months, three years, five years? And what could this then LEAD ON TO for the next 12months, three years, five years?

For the first time, technology has already overtaken us; it is growing quicker than we can keep up with! Earlier this year, I received a new mobile phone, and I don't just mean a new phone to me, or even a new phone (but one which has been out for a while) I mean ON THE DAY OF LAUNCH IN THE UK I had pre- ordered and received a BRAND NEW phone! I've never really gone in for the big red carpet launch stuff previously, but on this occasion, the marketing hype got the better of me, and I'd pre-ordered the brand new Samsung Galaxy S7 Edge and had one courier delivered to my house door at 8.07am the day it launched in the UK! I signed for the parcel, opened the packaging as if I were five years old and Santa had just answered my letter to him for Christmas! I excitedly pulled off the outer cellophane and turned on my brand new device for the very first time…….

The Samsung graphics swirls across the screen, the android logo popped up and popped back down again, the moment of truth...

"PLEASE WAIT WHILST WE DOWNLOAD 4 ESSENTIAL UPDATES!"

It was a brand new, fresh out of the box phone, on the morning of the launch, yet already technology had overtaken us, and was updating software fresh from the box!

So in our bid to achieve more we MUST be willing to review WHAT is required for us to achieve quicker, more succinctly, and how will technology play its part in assisting us to achieve that.

Therefore, I don't want you to restrict your thinking to what resource is available at present! At this stage why not open your mind to the possibility of what is yet to come! What might be possible? As a young child, I used to love watching to TV program 'Tomorrow's world' sharing with you prototypes and conceptions of what was yet to come. The Microwave oven, portable music devices, the mobile phone. At the time each program was aired these products were little more than concepts, prototypes at best, they were until they were shown on TV an idea, a concept, a vision as to what might be possible, and then someone or a group of people had gone about determining HOW that vision could become a reality.

I've recently read "Elon Musk: How the Billionaire CEO of SpaceX and Tesla is shaping our future" and just completely blown away by the man's vision, drive, and inspiration. From a troubled background in South Africa, during the apartheid, Elon has paid his way through a Pennsylvania education by turning his house into a club, and gone on to be responsible for things such as PayPal, SpaceX, Tesla and SpaceCity. With plans to enable colonies to be formed on MARS! He is another Steve Jobs in regards to vision, drive, and technology being at the forefront of his mind, but rather than ever say *"That can't be done"* has gone on to build the create and build the technology so that it may become possible!

What I'm trying to get at here, Is these visionaries are not constrained by current considerations as to whether the resources are available to achieve their goals, they look beyond the current into the 'what's possible' and then bring that 'future possibility' into the present! They manifest their future, by first visualising it, and then working backward to make the vision a reality!

So, when your thinking about the 'right equipment' for your next journey, don't stop at considering whether it's a car journey or a train ticket! Consider what OTHER means you MIGHT want to sample to get you from A to B!

It's far more important that having determined WHAT your utopia is, you then reverse engineer the process of what you need to do to achieve this than start out with a bag full of inspiration without any real idea as to where it might be leading you!

## Chapter 5 - The Busy-ness of Business

"Everything must be going well for you; you're always so busy!"

Remember that I shared with you my idea of utopia with the chateau and gites in France? Well, I don't remember including in there working 70,80,90+ hours per week managing the grounds, cleaning the pools, welcoming and booking in guests, providing food and entertainment, alongside the marketing, sales, invoicing and banking involved in running a multi-faceted business!

The thing is, I'm not planning to be there all the time, I've got a list twice as long as both my arm of places I'd like to visit, and 'other' things I'd like to do, and for all those who have read my book 'Battlefield2Boardroom' you'll know NOT to get me started on 'Bucket lists!'

However, all of these things will be required, IF I'm going to live within my idea of utopia, and so I'm also going to require a team of people working remotely to fulfill my idea of utopia.

I see countless numbers of Busy-ness owners, working harder and harder, longer and longer with this holy grail of an idea that 'One day, they'll have a successful business,' and THEN they'll be able to...

My most recent work as a keynote speaker is entitled "The road to utopia – and how to take a short cut" because I might not be here tomorrow!

A recent Google search quickly brought up the Forbes.com TOP 400 Billionaires! Which includes the 66 that were billionaires before they turned 40years old, and the Teenage Millionaire list!

Although disappointed to see there was not a woman in the top 10, I was pleased to see Lillian Bettencourt (L'Oreal) at number 11 and most interested to see Roman Abramovich currently ranked at number 151! Alongside six others with the same level of wealth!

The point I'm trying to make here is that there are people all around us, that are doing exceptionally well for themselves. People from all walks of life, all backgrounds, experiences, yet if I were to review ALL of them, the one common denominator amongst them all will be there vision, drive, and determination and the clarity of their vision.

**Learning to say NO**

For many entrepreneurs, learning to say "no" can be a trying experience. Far too often, you want to please everyone and do everything as soon as you can in hopes of increasing profits. It is imperative to learn early on that saying "no" can be as important, if not more so than saying "yes."

In our busy lives, as we look to please everyone, we often forget what's most important. For me, that's family, faith, health and my company. I use my dream board to keep me on the right track for the dreams I want to accomplish and to recognize which yeses will help me achieve those goals.

When deciding whether to respond with a "yes" or a "no," keep in mind: You can do anything, but you can't do everything.

Take a look here at how these four tips can help you remember why saying No is as important as saying YES to your business.

**Keep the clutter out**

The more you add to your plate, the less focus you have and the less attention you can pay to the things that matter to you. Don't let the distractions get the best of you. However, there are some that like a 'full plate' therefore ensure everything compliments everything else. Don't get side-tracked with anything, which ultimately doesn't contribute, to Utopia

1.     Don't dilute yourself

The more often you say yes, the more you dilute yourself, especially regarding your single most important focus. As you stretch yourself thinner by trying to do everything, you lose sight of your goals and may even get frustrated and burnt out. Can you simplify what it is YOU do? Can you train, share, pass over to, outsource, recruit, prevent, stop ANYTHING that doesn't require YOU to do it. Can you have such a simplified version of what it is YOU need to do, that every time you want to work, you do that thing! If you're a designer, then design and build a team of people around you to enable you to be the very best designer you can be.

2.     Seek help

Don't undertake something yourself that you know someone else might be able to dedicate their time to and do equally well.

Surround yourself with a great team that you can rely on to get the job done. Teams are exceptionally important, but not just a *"YES"* team. A *"YES"* team simply say Yes to you and anything else, they are 'keen little helpers, willing to do almost anything to HELP' well helping ISN'T saying YES all the time, Helping is about knowing when to say No, when to challenge and to hold to account to ensure we all remain 'on track' to achieve that audacious goal we first set out to achieve, not being swayed by 'shiny object syndrome' because they asked for some help!

3.     Think strategically

Saying "*No*" allows you to think strategically about the future. You may feel sure that you want something now, but you should evaluate how — and whether — it might benefit you in the future.

I've recently had one of the toughest decisions I've had to make (certainly within this business), and it was all about saying NO because of the business strategy!

When we launched My TrueNORTH, I assured everyone who attended that launch event that I would recognize and continue to do so those who joined on the day. Those who understand my vision, my focus, my plan and were willing to 'get onboard' and support us in supporting them from the very start. I've always maintained they shall be recognized as 'founder members' and treated accordingly.

However, what happens when one of your 'founder members', a significant contributor to your businesses own growth and a dedicated client, who has willingly recommended you to others, ceases to 'get' who you are and what it's all about. What happens when YOUR Utopia ceases to become theirs, and the longer your working together, the more evident it is that either one or the other is now compromising to maintain the business relationship! Something has to give! Someone has to be prepared to say No.

Our strategy is to provide the help, support, guidance, and accountability to business owners who are looking to significantly and sustainably grow them and their businesses. We do this through a range of methods from both group and 1:1 coaching/mentoring and by understanding WHAT it is that each client wishes to achieve and working with them to achieve it.

However, when they choose that the manner in which they intend to achieve their goals conflict with your understanding of ethics and morals you're left with two decisions, either amend your ethical stance to business and review your moral stance or be willing to say "Whilst I wish you every success, I'm afraid I'm no longer sure we can continue to add any further value to you or your business, and so suggest that we cease working together!"

This is not, you've got rotting teeth so that I won't sell you any more sweets here, (although you might argue it could be) it's about understanding WHO your ideal customers are, have been, can be and where YOU and YOUR business is heading. There are many who may have helped you get to WHERE YOU ARE. However, it is highly unlikely all of these shall be the ones who help you get to

WHERE YOU WANT TO BE! Whilst employment is often transitional, so are clients/customers!
Having everything right now can be fun, but it may not pay off in the long run. For it to work, (and continue to do so) part of our success is the ability to stay the course by saying "no" to some of the extras or perks that caught our eye early on but which may have damaged us and the company as we tried to grow.

Remember: Say "*No*" to things that may distract you from your goals and say "*Yes*" to what's most important to you and to achieving your goals.

I ran a course a while ago now entitled *"Time management for entrepreneurs"* the first time I ran the course, it was full of the same old people as you might expect to attend this type of training! The *"too busy to attend but I need to appear that I'm doing something about it"* ones, the *"I love courses, but do very little with what I've learnt"* ones and the *"Wanted to get out the office"* crowd, yet all three groups were AMAZED at what I taught!

You see this wasn't your bog standard 'time management' or 'time appreciation' training that everyone else was banging on about for the 'busy exec' this was specifically designed with the entrepreneur in mind, and the whole day was about doing less, and less and less; until you had narrowed down to the 1 or 2 things YOU HAD TO DO, without it affecting performance. This was the lazy entrepreneur's course; this was the *"say No, pass it back, automate, systemize, outsource, recruit and train"* version of time management, this was the *"where shall we holiday next*?" time management course, and it blew them off their feet!

Worldwide the current average 'life expectancy' is 71years. That's 852 months or 3,692 weeks or 25,932 days!

Now, based on the fact that I'm writing this at the age of 43 and nine months, that gives me 327months left before I'm on borrowed time! With that in mind my take on Time Management is significantly different to the person trying to talk about being in work on time and the knock on effect this can have on fellow workers!

Writing this book has so far cost me over 37 days of my time to research, review, consider and write! I've chosen to invest my time in this process because it brings me closer aligned to my vision, my utopia. But in doing so, I've also had to say "*No*" several times over to other things which would otherwise have been 'nice' but not contributed as much as this will to me achieving my goals.

We often talk about prioritizing tasks, jobs; 'to do' lists, etc., but when was the last time you took some time to prioritise your life!

### Chapter 6 - Mindset Mastery

Perception is Reality

Let me start this chapter by introducing you to my good friend Daniel. Daniel is one of the very best accountants I know. He's been an accountant for some time, won a whole series of industry awards and remains very passionate about his job. He invests both heavily and regularly into his own personal and professional development, and as such is a fully qualified, chartered accountant, with his successful practice and an exceptional reputation amongst his peers as being at the very forefront of accounting within the UK.

What is your perception of Dan so far? Is he a good guy?
Would you consider approaching him for some accountancy advice?

I guess that all depends on your perception of me, and whether my testimony to Dan's experience and expertise is to be trusted?

There is one other thing you ought to know about Dan, though...

Dan is an alcoholic!

So if you were to consider taking any accountancy advice from him, I'd recommend you did it before the pubs open at 11 am! Because by 3.30pm you might as well have asked the window cleaner!

Has your perception of Dan changed at all?

Based on the fact I started by giving Dan such a good testimony, has your perception of me changed at all?

You see the old expression *"You can't have a second chance at making a first impression"* has never been truer. We form an opinion, an impression of someone or something well before we have all the facts to base that opinion/impression on.

It is often reported that Henry Ford is quoted to have said this, however the actual quote originates far further back to Confucius who is reported to have stated *"The man who said I can, and the man who said I can't; shall invariably both prove to be right"* Henry Ford went on to say *"For the man who said "I can" shall find a way, whilst the man who said "I Can't" has already found an excuse!"*

A right-thinking, creative frame of mind is all it takes to achieve anything you desire. Being persistent in business will only make it easier to achieve your goals. Business is a domain that is unpredictable, but so is life. We don't know the result, but if you have a clear vision of the journey and what it is that you want out of your business, then you are pointed in the right direction to achieve that success.

You need passion to be able to venture into any project and business. Whether it is an extension of your home, finding the right schools for your children or wanting to be that successful businessperson. You need something that will encourage you to get up in the morning. If you're uneasy about going to work, then there's a problem. A possible lack of enthusiasm and passion for your business would be a likely scenario.

You need to stop now and re-think what it is that would make you interested again in your business. The last thing you want to do is work for the money only. There has got to be more than money that motivates you. The fact is if you don't offer your heart, soul and being persistent in business then you're likely not making the right business moves for growth and expansion.

Remember, if you're not ready to make business gains and help your customers, then somebody else will by take-over that business momentum that you once had and move into your territory! Now there's food for thought... would you let that happen to your business?

**Give New Strength to Clarity**

Along with passion, you need clarity. Being clear on your vision and plan will avoid a lot of unnecessary trial and errors. Not knowing how to reach your goal is like driving a car and not knowing the address of your destination. You can imagine the journey and how it would feel, but with no sense of direction or a clear path to your destination would be a very challenging journey.

Very rarely do you venture out of your front door without knowing where you are going? Most successful business people do their research, homework, and business planning by mapping and setting out a route to their business success. This way, you know where you are going, but also how long it will take to get there. You must bear in mind the obstacles and elements that may lay in your journeys path, and set aside some alternative paths should you require a diversion. If you are the business owner, guide and direct your team in the direction that you want to see yourself in the next six months or 5 years. The clarity of your business vision should filter down to every member of your team.

If the vision or the journey is too overwhelming, then break up the journey. Make shorter, achievable deadlines that you can reach as you travel along to the final destination. This will give you more clarity every step of the way until you reach your ultimate business goal.

**Ride the Business Tide**

The journey may be a pleasant, gradual ride for some businesses but for most start-up businesses this can be daunting. There will be a lot of obstacles in the way and people, who will naturally put them before you. Not everyone is a giving person. This can be disheartening and make you wonder why you took this journey in the first place. You may be losing money instead of making any, and this could go on for a long period.

Pull over, re-evaluate your business, what's going wrong and what's right? Don't continue until you have cleared your thoughts and the vision is transparent once again. In other words, use your 'side view mirrors' and 'windscreen wipers' to allow for a clear,

pleasant train of thought and journey. Don't forget, being persistent in business does pay off.

**Unparalleled Commitment**

Together with ongoing business evaluations, there is dedication that must play a major role on your part – Commitment. You need to be committed. If you don't have the commitment, you will withdraw physically and mentally from your daily tasks and not be able to achieve that success that you strive for.

Take a few steps back, or take some time out to gather your thoughts and grasp that your commitments were before they were side-stepped from the daily work humdrum.

You have invested a lot of time and finance into your business, whether it's new or old and therefore, you can't give up on the premise that you are mentally not capable of handling things at present. Again, you need to have vast control and authority and being organised in a way that makes you aware of all the 'ins' and 'outs' of your business. Be committed to being successful!

I'm sure we are all familiar with the expression *"Is the glass half empty or half full?"* determining people's perception to be either positive or negative, in order to manage our positive mind-set mastery we must spend time working on our positive mental outlook, the 'look for the silver lining' analogies and determine what lessons we can learn from anything that simply 'didn't go as we'd hoped or expected'

I'd like to conclude this chapter with just a little humour, so have included a longer list of 'The half empty glass analogies'!

- *The optimist says the glass is half full. The pessimist says the glass is half empty.*
- *The project manager says the glass is twice as big as it needs to be.*
- *The realist says the glass contains half the required amount of liquid for it to overflow.*
- *And the cynic... wonders who drank the other half The schoolteacher says it's not about whether the glass is half empty or half full, it's whether there is something in the glass at all.*
- *The ground-down mother of a persistently demanding five-year-old says sweetheart it's whatever you want it to be, just please let mummy have five minutes peace and quiet.*
- *The consultant says let's examine the question, prepare a strategy for an answer, and all for a daily rate of £X*
- *The inquisitive troublemaker wants to know what's in the glass anyhow*
- *The worrier frets that the remaining half will evaporate by next morning.*
- *And the entrepreneur sees the glass as undervalued by half its potential!!!!*

## Chapter 7 - Your Sherpa

Whilst you may have some people (Friends & Family, Neighbours, Colleagues, Employee's) all helping, supporting and encouraging you in your business...many business owners still never achieve their intended goals! They work harder and harder, strive more and more for that rich elixir of success, and despite 'giving it their all' fall short of their initial intended goals, left confused and frustrated as to why others can yet they have not!

And it is often simply because they don't have a Sherpa!
To paraphrase Albert Einstein, *"It takes a different kind of thinking to solve a problem than the kind of thinking which produced the problem"*
Who is also reported to have said *"If I only had one hour to save the world, I'd spend 59minutes thinking about the problem, and 1minute coming up with the solution"*

Since records began, man has been an explorer, an inventor, a maker, producer of things. The manner in which these have improved over time has been through this continuing cycle of exploration, invention, producing of improvements. We understand the importance of education greatly, and often speak of continual professional development, but the fact is some of the greatest lessons we will ever learn are currently being self-taught!

I remember some years ago now applying for an area managers post within a national organization. I'd updated my Curriculum Vitae, my covering letter demonstrated I'd done sufficient research on the company, the role and how I saw myself as an integral part of the project's success, and I was pleased to have been both invited to interview, and subsequently offered the position.

One of the questions at both application and interview stage was "Are you computer literate" to which I had responded "Exceptionally" however this had been sufficient for a 'tick to be placed in the box' and for us to move on with the interview and subsequently the job offer!

On day one, I have issued a smartphone, a laptop and tablet, a new email address and password into the companies' database! Setting all of these up, understanding how to use their system, their technology, their software, processes, and systems was pretty much left for me to work out for myself based on the fact I'd answered one question to say I considered myself computer literate!

Whether in sport or business, the means of getting from 'top of the Sunday league' to playing on the national team, determines more than skill, experience and being in the right place. When a professional football team stands on the pitch, there are tens if not a couple of hundred others that have enabled them to be therefore that game. From coach drivers and physiotherapists, from accountants to the providers of the kit, there is a whole myriad of people behind the team enabling them to concentrate on doing what they do best.

For each of those players to wear that jersey, they have also been coached through a process enabling to get to play at that level.

However, (and I say this most cautiously, as there are now an influx of people turning to coaching) there are many coaches that will keep you playing for Sunday League, keep telling you *"your not ready yet"*,*"just a few more weeks"*,*"once you have....."* and fewer that are encouraging you to make the big leaps forward to achieve SUCCESS!

Why is this? Why are coaches holding clients back from achieving all they are capable of? Well, (and I only speak from my observations) it's often commercial!

I'm not a great lover of systemized coaching. We've got this coaching system! It's often sold to retired bank managers and IFA's as a means of being able to continue earning after they are retired off from corporate land!

Yes I know they have spent 35,40,45 years *"in business"* they have been *"working with business owners"* all of their lives, and there is *"nothing you can tell me about business, I haven't heard before!"*

You see, pick the wrong coach, and it's often because they are in it for them! Pick a coach with a business plan that says 'this will do me until I'm 65 years old' approach, and you can pretty much guarantee your business plan will come to fruition about the same time as they turn 65!

I expect all of my clients to be transitional; I need them to be because those gites aren't for my coaching clients either! No- where in my vision of utopia does it allow for the people I'm currently working with!

The RIGHT coach should be able to provide personalised guidance that helps take you from where you are now to where you want to be, In the shortest amount of time possible.

Successful people weren't perfect on day one. They got that way out of HABIT. And habits are built day by day. No one was born with great habits, yet everyone can develop them.

YOUR COACH should help you identify, install, and maintain the habits that will change your life so you can earn more money, advance your career, improve your business, improve your relationships, or just feel happier and more fulfilled.

I heard a lovely expression a number of years ago, and have used it ever since *"The most expensive advice you'll ever take, is given for free, by a poor and busy fool"* again it's not intended to sound heartless or uncaring, but the number of people I hear asking or taking advice from people who don't know them, their circumstances, their business or and most importantly their goals and how this advice is likely to affect those goals!

*"If I were you..."* they often say, and often with the very best intent. I'm not trying to say all those who give advice are fools, but it's rarely the best advice when it starts *"If I were you..."* because of your not!

It was Jim Rohan who is reported to have been the first to say *"Who you hang around with matters, A LOT"* although many others have followed suit and made similar comments. The fact is you should frequently consider who you are 'hanging around' and getting advice from. Too many people have their agenda, their opinion means more to them than anyone else and although they 'mean well' can simply distort your vision or your utopia. Getting advice, help, support, guidance, coaching, mentoring whatever else is the right thing to do if you truly want to become the very best version of you that you can be.

However an advert in the local paper, is unlikely to reveal the right person to you, you need to build a relationship with someone who genuinely wants the best for you, and is willing to review as to whether sharing this bit of the journey together is positive and likely to be productive for both of you!

**Chapter 8 - Too big for your boots!**

The fear of failure can often stagnate business owners thinking, and creativity. However, the fear of success is just as predominant (if not more so in quick to grow businesses) and thus prevents a willingness to try new things or continue to pursue new opportunities.

One of the most common business phenomena is also one of the most perplexing: when successful companies face big changes in their environment, they often fail to respond effectively. Unable to defend themselves against competitors armed with new products, technologies, or strategies, they watch their sales and profits erode, their best people leave, and their stock valuations tumble. Some ultimately manage to recover—usually after painful rounds of downsizing and restructuring—but many don't.

**Why do good companies go bad?**

It's often assumed that the problem is paralysis. Confronted with a disruption in business conditions, companies freeze; they're caught like the proverbial deer in the headlights. But that explanation doesn't fit the facts. In studying once-thriving companies that have struggled in the face of change, little evidence has been found of paralysis; quite the contrary. The managers of besieged companies usually recognize the threat early, carefully analyze its implications for their business, and unleash a flurry of initiatives in response. For all the activity, though, the companies still falter.

The problem is not an inability to take action but an inability to take appropriate action. There can be many reasons for the problem—ranging from owner/managerial stubbornness to sheer incompetence—but one of the most common is a condition that I call active inertia.

Active inertia is an organization's tendency to follow established patterns of behaviour—even in response to dramatic environmental shifts. Stuck in the modes of thinking and working that brought success in the past, market leaders simply accelerate all their tried-and-true activities. In trying to dig themselves out of a hole, they just deepen it.

Because active inertia is so common, it's important to understand its sources and symptoms. After all, if executives assume that the enemy is paralysis, they will automatically conclude that the best defense is action. But if they see that action itself can be the enemy, they will look more deeply into all their assumptions before acting.

They will, as a result, gain a clearer view of what needs to be done and, equally important, what may prevent them from doing it. And they will significantly reduce the odds of joining the ranks of fallen leaders.

**Victims of Active Inertia**

To see the destructive potential of active inertia, consider the examples of Firestone Tire & Rubber and Laura Ashley. Both companies were leading players in their industries, and both failed to meet the challenge of change—not because they didn't act but because they didn't act appropriately.

As Firestone entered the 1970s, it was enjoying seven decades of uninterrupted growth. It sat atop the thriving U.S. tire industry, alongside Goodyear, its crosstown rival in Ohio. Firestone's managers had a clear vision of their company's positioning and strategy. They saw the Big Three Detroit automakers as their key customers; they saw Goodyear and the other leading U.S. tire makers as their competitors, and they saw their challenge as simply keeping up with the steadily increasing demand for tires.

The company had become a monument to its success. Its culture and operations reflected the vision of its founder, Harvey Firestone, Sr., who insisted on treating customers and employees as part of the "Firestone family." The Firestone Country Club was open to all employees, regardless of rank, and Harvey himself maintained close friendships with the top executives of the big carmakers. (In fact, his granddaughter married Henry Ford's grandson.)

Firestone created fiercely loyal managers, steeping them in the company's family values and its worldview.

The company's operating and capital allocation processes were designed to exploit the booming demand for tires by quickly bringing new production capacity online. In the capital-budgeting process, for example, frontline employees identified market opportunities and translated them into proposals for investing in additional capacity. Middle managers then selected the most promising proposals and presented them to top executives, who tended to speedily approve the middle managers' recommendations.

Firestone's long-standing success gave the company a strong, unified sense of its strategies and values, its relationships with customers and employees, and its operating and investment processes. The company had, in short, a clear formula for success, which had served it well since the turn of the century.

Then, almost overnight, everything changed. A French company, Michelin, introduced the radial tire to the U.S. market. Based on a breakthrough in design, radials were safer, longer-lasting, and more economical than traditional bias tires. They had already come to dominate European markets, and when Ford declared in 1972 that all its new cars would have radials, it was clear that they would dominate the U.S. market, too.

Firestone was not taken by surprise by the arrival of radials. Through its large operations in Europe, it had witnessed first-hand the European markets' quick embrace of radial tires during the 1960s. And it had developed forecasts that clearly indicated that radials would be rapidly accepted by U.S. automakers and consumers as well. Firestone saw radials coming, and it swiftly took action: it invested nearly $400 million—more than $1 billion in today's dollars—in radial production, building a new plant dedicated to radial tires and converting several existing factories. Although Firestone's response was quick, it was far from effective. Even as it invested in the new product, it clung to its old ways of working. Rather than redesign its production processes, it just tinkered with them—even though the manufacture of radial tires required much higher quality standards. Also, the company delayed closing many of its factories that produced bias tires, despite clear indications of their impending obsolescence. Active inertia had taken hold.

By 1979, Firestone was in deep trouble. Its plants were running at an anemic 59% of capacity, it was renting warehouses to store unsold tires, it was plagued by costly and embarrassing product recalls, and its domestic tire business had burned more than $200 million in cash. Although overall U.S. tire sales were plateauing, largely because of radials last twice as long as bias tires, Firestone's CEO clung to the assumption of ever-growing demand, telling the board that he saw no need to start closing plants. In the end, all of Firestone's intense analysis and action was for zero return. The company surrendered much of its share of the U.S. market to foreign corporations, and it suffered through two hostile takeover bids before finally being acquired by Bridgestone, a Japanese company, in 1988.

In my second example, the women's apparel maker Laura Ashley also fell victim to active inertia. The company's eponymous founder spent her youth in Wales, and she started the business with her husband, Bernard, in 1953 as a way to re-create the mood of the British countryside. The company's garments, designed to evoke a romantic vision of English ladies tending roses at their country manors, struck a chord with many women in the 1970s.

The business grew quickly from a single silk-screen press in Laura and Bernard's London flat to a major retailer with a network of 500 shops and a powerful brand the world over.

Laura Ashley expanded her tiny operation not to maximize profits but to defend and promote traditional British values, which she felt were under siege from sex, drugs, and miniskirts in the 1960s. From the beginning, she and Bernard exercised tight control over all aspects of the business, keeping design, manufacturing, distribution, and retailing in-house. The couple opened a central manufacturing and distribution centre in Wales, and they proudly labelled their garments "Made in Wales." They provided generous wages and benefits to their employees, thereby avoiding the labour unrest that crippled many British industries throughout the 1970s. They also established close relationships with their franchisees and customers, who grew fiercely loyal to the company's products and the values they embodied.

When Laura died in 1985, Bernard kept the company on the course his wife had set. Fashion, however, changed. As more women entered the workforce, they increasingly chose practical, professional attire over Laura Ashley's more romantic garments. Competitors publicly dismissed the Laura Ashley style as better suited to milkmaids in the 1880s than CEOs in the 1980s. At the same time, apparel manufacturing was undergoing a transformation. With trade barriers falling, fashion houses were rushing to move production offshore or to outsource it entirely, dramatically reducing their operating costs. Laura Ashley, in contrast, continued to pursue the out-dated designs and the expensive manufacturing processes that had served it so well in the past.

The company did not, however, suffer from paralysis. By the late 1980s, an outside consultant had identified the major challenges facing Laura Ashley and had outlined remedial actions.

Recognising the need to act, the board of directors, chaired by Bernard, brought in a series of new CEOs, asking each to develop and carry out a restructuring plan that would increase sales and cut costs. The new plans set off flurries of activity, but none of them went far enough in recasting the company's strategy. It remained unclear whether Laura Ashley was a brand, a manufacturer, a retailer, or an integrated fashion company. Nor did the plans refresh the company's traditional values to bring them in line with the marketplace. Afflicted with active inertia, Laura Ashley went through seven CEOs in a decade, but the company's decline continued. American televangelist Pat Robertson joined the board as an outside director, leading one financial journal to conclude that the company sought divine inspiration for its earthly problems.

**The Four Hallmarks of Active Inertia**
To understand why successful companies like Firestone and Laura Ashley fail, it is necessary to examine the origins of their success. Most leading businesses owe their prosperity to a fresh competitive formula—a distinctive combination of strategies, processes, relationships, and values that set them apart from the crowd. As the formula succeeds, customers multiply, talented workers flock to apply, investors bid up the stock, and competitors respond with the sincerest form of flattery— imitation. All this positive feedback reinforces managers' confidence that they have found the one best way, and it emboldens them to focus their energies on refining and extending their winning system.
 The fresh thinking that led to a company's initial success is often replaced by a rigid devotion to the status quo.

Frequently, though, the system begins to harden. The fresh thinking that led to a company's initial success is replaced by a rigid devotion to the status quo. And when changes occur in the company's markets, the formula that had brought success instead brings failure.

The Dynamic of Failure Leading companies can become stuck in the modes of thinking and working that brought them their initial success. When business conditions change, their once-winning formulas instead bring failure.

## The failure to be flexible

When strategic frameworks, systems, and processes become rigid, companies, just like nations, tend to keep fighting the last war. When Xerox's management surveyed the competitive battlefield in the 1970s, it saw IBM and Kodak as the enemy, its 40,000 sales and service representatives as its troops, and its patented technologies as its insurmountable defenses. Xerox's strategic work frames enabled the company to fight off traditional foes using established tactics and to rebuff repeated attempts by IBM and Kodak to attack its core market. But the strategic frames blinded Xerox to the new threat posed by guerrilla warriors such as Canon and Ricoh, which were targeting individuals and small companies for their high-quality compact copiers.

Once Xerox's management recognized the magnitude of the threat from the new entrants, it belatedly but aggressively launched a series of quality programs designed to beat the Japanese at their own game.

These initiatives did stem Xerox's share loss and the company's victory over the Japanese was trumpeted in books with titles like Xerox: American Samurai. The focus on beating the Japanese, however, distracted Xerox's management from the emerging battle for the personal computer. At the time, Xerox's Palo Alto research centre was pioneering several of the technologies that sparked the personal computer revolution, including the graphical user interface and the mouse. But Xerox was unable to capitalize on the new opportunities because they lay outside its strategic frames.

## Processes harden into routines.

When a company decides to do something new, employees usually try several different ways of carrying out the activity. But once they have found a way that works particularly well, they have strong incentives to lock into the chosen process and stop searching for alternatives. Fixing on a single process frees people's time and energy for other tasks. It leads to increased productivity, as employees gain experience performing the process. And it also provides the operational predictability necessary to coordinate the activities of a complex organization.

But just as with strategic work frames, established processes often take on a life of their own. They cease to be a means to an end and become ends in themselves. People follow the processes not because they're effective or efficient but because they're well known and comfortable. They are simply "the way things are done." Once a process becomes a routine, it prevents employees from considering new ways of working. Alternative processes never get considered, much less tried. Active inertia sets in.

I recently had a need to hire a van for a day. The beauty of the Internet these days is everything can be done online, so a quick search and I could see at a glance as to the cost, distance, and availability of the various options available to me.

I didn't automatically opt for the cheapest. It was a local, independent firm and for the sake of £6 more, I didn't want to run the risk of getting there to find a problem, so plumped for the internationally recognised brand Europcar.

Their website enabled me to input all my driving details, and 'check in online' just like an airport to 'minimise delay on collecting the vehicle' Full payment was made, and I immediately received paperwork within my inbox to confirm the hire some four days later.

However, just 20minutes before the hire period was due to begin (and some 8 miles from the hire venue) I received a call from their 'Head office' to be advised they were *"Having problems locating a van for my hire, and would not be available when I arrived*!" On arrival at the venue to determine what had gone wrong I was advised, they have X amount of vans in their fleet, and allow the same amount to be hired out, WITHOUT ANY CONSIDERATION as to where-a-about in the country these vans are or being returned to, or without consideration for those who may have an accident, break down or simply wish to extend their hire! Not only was this a problem for me, but for two other people who had also reserved vans for that day from this location, and would not be able to continue with their hire! Apparently, two previous customers had returned the vans to 'other locations' and would take the time to re- locate back to this site, and another had simply called to extend their hire!

When I asked about the paperwork I had received stating YOUR VEHICLE IS NOW CONFIRMED I was advised, **"Yeah well, we've always done it like that!"**

The systems and processes they had when it was a lot smaller a lot less busy and a lot easier to manage people's bookings had not been updated or reviewed to correspond with the ability to now book online (even though they have had this feature for over 6 years) and as such not only this site but EVERY SITE IN THE COUNTRY were often receiving these problems when vans were not being returned on time, in working condition or to the same site as was booked from!

McDonald's is another example of a company whose routines have dulled its response to shifting market conditions. In the early 1990s, the fast-food giant's operations manual comprised 750 pages detailing every aspect of a restaurant's business. For years, the company's relentless focus on standardized processes, all dictated by headquarters, had allowed it to rapidly roll out its winning formula in the market after market, ensuring the consistency and efficiency that attracted customers and dismayed rivals.

By the 1990s, however, McDonald's was in a rut. Consumers were looking for different and healthier foods, and competitors such as Burger King and KFC were capitalizing on the shift in taste by launching new menu items. McDonald's, however, was slow to respond to the changes. Its historical strength—a single-minded focus on refining its mass-production processes—turned into a weakness.

By requiring menu decisions to pass through headquarters, the company stifled innovation and delayed action. Its central development kitchen, removed from the actual restaurants and their customers, churned out a series of products, such as the McPizza, McLean, and Arch Deluxe, but they all failed to entice diners.

**Relationships become shackles**

To succeed, every company must build strong relationships—with employees, customers, suppliers, lenders, and investors. Laura and Bernard Ashley worked diligently to win the hearts of new customers, franchisees, and investors at every step of their company's expansion. Harvey Firestone, Sr., maintained close friendships with his customers, provided loans out of his pocket to struggling tire dealers during the Great Depression, and socialized with many of his company's top executives.

When conditions shift, however, companies often find that their relationships have turned into shackles, limiting their flexibility and leading them into active inertia. The need to maintain existing relationships with customers can hinder companies in developing new products or focusing on new markets.

Kirin Brewery, for example, gained control of a daunting 60% share of the post-war Japanese beer market by building strong relationships with people in business, many of whom had received the company's lager as part of their rations in the army. In the 1980s, Kirin was reluctant to alienate its core customers by offering the trendy dry beer favoured by younger drinkers. Kirin's slow response allowed Asahi Breweries to catch up and then surpass it as the industry leader.

Managers can also find themselves constrained by their relationships with employees, as the saga of Apple Computer vividly illustrates. Apple's vision of technically elegant computers and its freewheeling corporate culture attracted some of the most creative engineers in the world, who went on to develop a string of smash products including the Apple II, the Macintosh, and the PowerBook. As computers became commodities, Apple knew that its continued health depended on its ability to cut costs and speed up a time to market. Imposing the necessary discipline, however, ran counter to the Apple culture, and top management found itself frustrated whenever it tried to exert more control.
The engineers simply refused to change their ways. The relationships with creative employees that enabled Apple's early growth ultimately hindered it from responding to environmental changes.

The business you are in right now also deserves to become the very best version of it that it can be. This means it should never be prevented from growing, developing and moving with the demand for your product/service.

However, to prevent any of the examples I have listed above, it is imperative that the mission and vision of the business are flexible enough to work with the current and future trends of your current customers, and not create systems and processes so entrenched in the here and now that it prevents the development of initiative and continues to embrace technology and the fluidity of customer trends and spends!

**Chapter Nine - It Ends with Grit and Determination**

*"Nothing in this world can take the place of persistence.*
*Talent will not:*
*Nothing is more common than unsuccessful men with talent.*
*Genius will not:*
*Unrewarded genius is almost a proverb.*
*Education will not:*
*The world is full of educated derelicts.*
*Persistence and determination alone are omnipotent."*
**Phil Calvert – Former All Blacks Rugby Captain**

When I first read this quote, I was a college student studying Psychology, Sociology, and Politics I didn't quite grasp the magnitude of what persistence and determination would mean to me. Or how successful people don't have greater luck than others. They work hard to create and seize opportunities that drive them towards achieving goals with a clear vision.

This applies to both our personal and professional lives. No matter what success means to the individual, studies show that those who exhibit more "grit" and persistence have a better chance of reaching milestones and exceeding personal goals.

And guess what? Grit, like many other competencies, is something that can be developed with practice. Later, and after I had finished my formative education, I joined the British Army, and studied to become an Advanced Trauma Medic.

As a medic, you are often 'loaned' to whoever requires that particular set of advanced skills, then moved back into a 'pool' ready to be 'loaned' again as required.

Over time, I became more and more fascinated with the parachute regiment high-performance culture and never-quit mentality. I realized that outside of participating in sports such as swimming and rugby and having hobbies like skydiving; they were continually testing and re-evaluating their limits. I had never set and achieved a goal that seemed totally insurmountable. So one day, and without giving it too much thought, I had an epiphany. I was going to become the very best advanced trauma medic I could be and become capable of being 'loaned' to the number of specialist rapid deployment regiments within the British Armed Forces.

My outlook had changed, my regime changed, my results changed. I lost any excessive weight I'd been carrying for a while, I began to exercise EVERY day, I studied harder, longer, more intensely and began volunteering for exercises, deployments and operational tours I would not otherwise have considered.

I started realising that the mental and physical aspects of becoming more "*gritty*" are not mutually exclusive. One's mind could be strengthened by pushing the body beyond perceived limits. That mental strength could then be leveraged to overcome other types of obstacles.

I deployed several times on operational commitments all over the world, often supporting specialist rapid deployment troops, and worked to the very best of my ability to ensure everyone who went out, came home.

Since leaving the Army, after a medical discharge in 2003, I have again required a significant amount of grit and determination to overcome 'civilian attitude' to my medical diagnosis with Post Traumatic Stress Disorder!

I again learned that determination carried more weight than intelligence and talent. I also spent several years during this time as a non-domicile but very dedicated single parent to a young, growing and at times very challenging son! I am not sure which was harder, that, or basic training!

During the times when I wanted to lock myself in my room and scream, I would reflect on the Corps motto of the Royal Army Medical Corps – In Ardius Fidelius Faithful throughout adversity" I can't think of a single successful entrepreneur who hasn't experienced hardship along the way. Those that learn to manage fear, push forward and navigate the inevitable obstacles ultimately find success.

I know there will be many more tests in this life that will require grit and determination to come out on the other side stronger and wiser. But there are four pieces of advice I would offer:

1.      **Find purpose in everything you do**. Otherwise, what's the point? The most successful people love what they do and feel

Connected to a purpose, they believe to be greater than them. They lead change, innovate and find ways to make the world a better place even if it's in the smallest way.

2.      **Connect that purpose to your values**. I get it. Sometimes we just need to get a job, pay the bills and keep moving forward despite life's many obstacles. Throughout my many experiences, though, I have found one commonality regardless of what "job" someone is in. The happiest people find ways to think about their lives and careers in ways other than what you would find in a job description. Find links between what you do and more importantly, why.

3.      **Develop an optimistic outlook**. Mental fortitude is what gets you through in the Armed Forces both on and off the battlefield. It keeps you vigilant in combat; it helps the strong overcome illnesses; it's the foundation for successful business leaders. Negativity is not only pointless, but it completely inhibits one's ability to maintain focus on specific goals. It clouds the once clear vision. Don't get distracted by the pitfalls. Leap over them in the sole pursuit of your goals.

4.      **Silence the inner critic**. We all have one. Ignore it. Getting outside of our comfort zones is when the real magic starts to happen. Another one of our many sayings in the Army is "Get comfortable being uncomfortable." The more we push ourselves beyond what we think are our limits, the larger that comfort zone becomes. Then things that used to seem impossible become part of our everyday lives.

Be all in, all the time. Embrace every day as it comes. Face adversity and smile; I'm alive, and therefore today is already a good day! There is no greater feeling than knowing you leave everything you have on the battlefield of life.

## Chapter Ten - My TrueNORTH

My TrueNORTH was formally launched in May 2015, although the philosophy had been forming for some 7-8 years before the formal launch of business.

You see, since leaving the British Army through medical discharge, after having served for over 12 years, I initially struggled to gain employment. I have good qualifications, great experience, and some wonderful references, yet the reason for such a difficulty in gaining employment was other people's perception of my medical discharge! Although I'd been in the hospital, I'd been treated, fully recovered, had been 'signed as fit to return to work' yet was virtually unemployable! And simply because it wasn't a physical injury that had seen me hospitalised for so long, but a mental illness! I was diagnosed with Post Traumatic Stress Disorder (PTSD) and had been sectioned under the mental health act 'for my protection.' This single factor was the largest hurdle to ever seeking 'valuable' employment as the fear and uncertainty of those I shared this with, was sufficient to quickly change their attitude from 'on paper, he's a good catch' to 'long-term sickness absence risk.'

With little other option, I was almost forced to set up my own business simply as a means of generating income, as employment appears unattainable! It wasn't long at all before I discovered both my military skills and experiences were VERY relevant to the required skills of business, and as the business grew and grew, any thought of employment was quickly replaced with becoming an employer!

Since 2004, I've found by applying myself 'differently' to those around me I've always had a different result. By being willing to maintain that role of 'service' I learned through the military has enabled me to build more, better and more productive relationships with prospects, clients, suppliers, competitors even. By maintaining an attitude of "How, can I help you?" as opposed to "What's in it for me?" has always proven to be a far more successful strategy and one, which I thoroughly recommend.

I was previously head hunted and subsequently worked for a national company providing business growth advice to its members. There was a vibrant team, and we collectively had an amazing job opportunity to help business owners significantly grow their businesses. I picked my hours, managed my designated area the way I saw fit and had the freedom to work in a manner of my choosing.

However, something was wrong, and over a period of months that feeling grew and grew to the extent that despite having raised my observations and concerns something had to be DONE!

You see, our success as employees, our objectives, and our bonus structure was based around P&L, not of our member's growth and success!

Now I do understand and accept EVERY business needs to grow. But the act of service to its clients was changing.

Internal dialogue shifted from Member to Membership; the emphasis moved from Person to Pound. Instead of being measured on the effectiveness of the guidance and support we provided to our members and THEIR growth, the emphasis was on our P&L account and the continual upsell of other products and services for OUR business growth, and as a result, the business was growing broke!

My TrueNORTH is an Ethical Coaching Consultancy, supporting savvy business owners to significantly and sustainably grow both them and their businesses. We pride ourselves on being absolutely client focused, by ensuring we continually consider our client's goals and objectives alongside our own and be willing to advise and recommend to clients accordingly if their goals are not aligned with our own!

It's about a continual act of service to first understand and then continually support, encourage and guide others towards their success summit, their Utopia, it's about our goals BEING to see others succeed in theirs, it's about being willing to ask the difficult questions maybe nobody else will ensure you remain on course to achieve your TrueNORTH!

We do this in a series of ways, from online products and group coaching; through to 1:1 mentorship and Mastermind Groups, and the results we continue to witness are amazing.

*"I've got more value from 1 hour with Jay than I have from a year with my previous coach, it's been transformational for both me and my business. It was a barrage of idea's thought, suggestions.*
*All were up to date, relevant and easy to apply there and then to make a marked different in the way we do business, I wish I'd met Jay years ago."*
**Jo Wright - Training Company**

*"In my dealings with Jay and the team at My TrueNORTH, I found them to always be very focused on and attentive to my needs. The kindness, encouragement, and support that they gave me during our sessions proved to be most valuable to me and were certainly of great help in enabling me to manage my situation.*
*In particular, Jay encouraged me to develop and expand my perspectives about how I address obstacles. I found his ethical approach to coaching more endearing; he came across as being genuinely interested in my development, a refreshing change and I am very happy to endorse him and his coaching/mentorship abilities and wish him and his business every success."*
**Phil Loxton – Language Consultant**

*"Jay is Mr. Motivator - he knows how to spur people on and get the best from them. At times we all can have a tough time, the last time I did; was particularly tough, but I knew who to turn to! I've worked with Jay many times now and shall continue to do so. He also comes highly recommended in my book."*

**Liz Ward – Boutique Legal Practice**

*"By working with Jay, My TrueNORTH and the mastermind group Our 2015 Q4 ROI is up 1100% against the same period in 2014, which is insane! - Thank you, Thank you, Thank you."*

**Greg Jones - Online Retailer**

If you have been inspired by what you have read, if you are intrigued by anything I have shared, if you have found the text to excite, embrace and motivate your entrepreneurial spirit; I'd be delighted to hear from you.

Visit: **www.MyTrueNORTH.Biz/Book**

Made in the USA
Charleston, SC
04 January 2017